The Talking Stick Volume 23

Symmetry

The Talking Stick Volume 23

Symmetry

A publication of the
Jackpine Writers' Bloc

Managing Editors: Sharon Harris and Tarah L Wolff
Copy Editors: Sharon Harris, Jerry Mevissen, Anne Morgan, Marilyn Wolff
Layout and Production: Tarah L Wolff
Editorial Board: Marlys Guimaraes, Sharon Harris, Jerry Mevissen, Anne Morgan,
Tarah L Wolff

This publication is made possible, in part, by a grant from Itasca-Mantrap
Co-op. Electrical Association through Operation Round Up.

Send correspondence to Jackpine Writers' Bloc, 13320 149th Avenue, Menahga, MN
56464. sharrick1@wcta.net.

ISBN: 978-1-928690-26-9

Table of Contents

Table of Contents

Table of Contents

Table of Contents

Co-Editor's Note - Sharon Harris

Editor's Choice: "Celebration" (p.167) by Marlys Guimaraes

My Editor's Choice this year is "Celebration" by Marlys Guimaraes, p. 167. Marlys lost her mother shortly before I lost my own. She expressed many things that I also felt after this loss of such magnitude. Our loved ones can die a quiet death, small in the whole scheme of things, but so huge, so important in our lives. Her poem was a stunning description of the departed being greeted by their loved ones. This indeed is a celebration.

Things are changing in my world and I do not do well with change or with letting go. I am always telling myself that change has to happen— otherwise, the bad things in life won't change and go away either. My beloved niece is remodeling my parents' old house, the house where my sister and I grew up. This is going to be hard. I know it will end up new and beautiful inside but watching it change to get there will be rough. We have discussed how, as she and her boyfriend are tearing down walls, removing old plaster and lath, they are uncovering all the parts of the old house that Mother and Dad saw as they were first remodeling that house, enclosing part of the screened-in porch, making new rooms, creating a new life for themselves. Now we can actually see that the house was once just a square two-story house. We can see the old roof line and the old siding from the original house before someone added on the screened-in porch on two sides. We are seeing what Mother and Dad saw, all those decades ago, the bare bones of what they started with when they were young and full of dreams and plans. As parts of the old house are uncovered, we get a glimpse back to the time when they had a whole long future ahead of them with love and work and family and good neighbors all around.

People meet and make a life for themselves, never knowing how long that life will be, how sad or glad, how much they will grow and learn and change. Sometimes the end of life can be sad and empty and lonely, so little family left, neighbors gone. It is good to remember back and see what our parents saw, imagine the paths they walked, see the hidden layers of their lives, and honor their journey. And always, always, we need to record their stories. This remodeling of my parents' house has become, in my mind, a celebration of their life, their love, and our childhood years.

Co-Editor's Note - Tarah L Wolff

Editor's Choice: "My Youngest Uncle" (p.48) by Kathryn Knudson

Right now I am currently living in a world surrounded by stories of those that came before me and the lives of those that I have lost. My friends and other authors have learned that this year I may be surrounded by stories, but I will not be writing. Next year I may get to be a writer again but this year I am a contractor.

I am renovating my grandparents' one hundred year old farm house. Words are everywhere—in the empty Mason jars, in the abandoned work benches and in the discarded cabinets that I could not save that they built themselves. I am glad that this wasn't someone else's house cared for by hands I had never held nor stories I had never heard but there is stinging knowledge too. I know why those Mason jars sat empty for so long. There is no way in this labor for me to paint a brighter fiction with my imagination. No, I know all of the stories here—how they laughed, worked and loved and also the last painful final endings. The sting sometimes makes me wish that this had been a house lived in by strangers, as then, perhaps, an empty Mason jar would not make me so sad.

My editor's choice this year will probably not surprise you when you read it as it is a glimpse into a family, a memory and a hard time. It is amazing how few words are capable of breaking a person's heart. I was alone one night, hot, exhausted (framing in a wall) when I sat down in the lonely and felt so depleted and so empty in the now-fully-gutted shell that was my grandparents' house. I remembered the nine years my grandma lived here alone after she lost my grandpa and it gave me strength. Both of my grandmas lived without their men for years upon years, a common thing I suppose but that does not lessen the sting. I wondered if this house felt as empty to her then as it did to me in that moment and I also knew how she got through the silent hours. She just did.

Her blood runs in my veins and it feels right to keep it here. I see her hands in my hands and, sometimes, it feels like she's getting to do this all over again. Pick out the cabinets and the hardware and the paint colors. Choose the right floors to take the burden of family, friends and the rest of our lives. Here she is in me, a writer, continuing her story in the beginning of my own.

Judges

Margaret Hasse, Poetry Judge

Margaret Hasse is author of four collections of poems, including *Earth's Appetite*, which was published in 2013. She has received grants and awards for her poetry from the National Endowment of the Arts, The Loft-McKnight Fellowship, Jerome Foundation, and Minnesota State Arts Board. Two of her books were finalists for the Minnesota Book Award. Her collection *Milk and Tides* won the poetry award from the Midwest Independent Publishers Association.

Mary Carroll Moore, Creative Nonfiction Judge

Mary Carroll Moore, M.A., M.F.A., is a writing coach and teacher, book doctor for publishing houses, author of thirteen books, and a formerly nationally syndicated columnist for the *Los Angeles Times* and 86 other newspapers. Over 300 of her articles, essays, short stories, and poems have appeared in literary journals, magazines, and newspapers around the U.S. She is currently on the faculty of Grub Street Writing School in Boston, Massachusetts, the Hudson Valley Writers Center in Westchester County, New York, the Loft Literary Center in Minneapolis, Minnesota, and Madeline Island School of the Arts in LaPointe, Wisconsin.

Peter Geye, Fiction Judge

Peter Geye is the award-winning author of *Safe From the Sea*, now being made into a motion picture. He also wrote *The Lighthouse Road*, which was a finalist for the Midwest Booksellers Choice Award and the Midwest Society of Authors Award for fiction and winner of the Northeastern Minnesota Book Award, and was selected as a World Book Night selection in 2014. He has a Ph.D. from Western Michigan University, where he was editor of *Third Coast*. He lives in Minneapolis and is at work on a new novel.

Winners

Poetry 1st Place

"Letting the Geraniums Die" (p.1) by Kit Rohrbach

Kit's poetry and prose has appeared in several regional publications including *The Talking Stick, Lake Region Review* and the annual Poet/Artist Collaboration at Crossings in Zumbrota. She lives, writes, and herds cats in Rochester, Minnesota.

Creative Nonfiction 1st Place

"One Almost Cleared the Pasture Fence" (p.2) by Mim Kagol

Mim is 68 years old, a retired English teacher (35 years), a wife, mother, and grandmother. She lives in a suburb of Minneapolis with her husband and cat. She is passionate about reading and writing, loves to quilt, knit prayer shawls, travel, and care for her aging mother. Mim is active in several charitable foundations. She finds poems everywhere and sometimes she even writes them down. She has had her poetry published in *The Talking Stick* in the past. This is her first published creative nonfiction.

Fiction 1st Place

"Walking the Line" (p.5) by Cheyenne Marco

Cheyenne is currently working on her M.A. in creative writing at the University of South Dakota where she teaches introductory college writing and literature. Her work has appeared in the third edition of the *Lake Region Review*, and she has read her works at the John R. Milton Writer's Conference and Southwest Minnesota State's and the Minnesota State Colleges' and Universities' undergraduate research conferences.

2nd Place and Honorable Mention

Poetry 2nd Place:
Audrey Kletscher Helbling
"Sunday Afternoon at the Auction Barn" (p.8)

Poetry Honorable Mention:
Marlene Mattila Stoehr "The Visit" (p.150)
Janice Larson Braun "The Gift" (p.15)
David Eric Northington "Regret" (p.95)
Thomas C Stetzler "Twilight Crossing" (p.111)
Marilyn Wolff "Progression" (p.51)

Creative Nonfiction 2nd Place:
Charmaine Pappas Donovan
"Skating the Edge of Memory" (p.9)

Creative Nonfiction Honorable Mention:
Mike Lein "My North Woods Persona" (p.105)
Andrea Taylor Langworthy "The Grand March" (p.165)
Cheyenne Marco "Minnesota Smoke" (p.25)

Fiction 2nd Place:
Chet Corey
"Those Long Winter Mornings" (p.10)

Fiction Honorable Mention:
Paisley Kauffmann "Josephine" (p.29)
Deb Schlueter "Fireweed" (p.79)

The Talking Stick Volume 23

Symmetry

Letting Geraniums Die

Poetry Winner • Kit Rohrbach

There is no sign
between one time
and the next.
The peppery, powdery smell
of geranium leaves
is the same now
as it was in summer.
A few more leaves are yellow,
a few more white petals
fall like a forecast
when I touch them.
The dirt in the pot is dry.

In spring, shoeless, sleeveless,
I dippered water
above my head, let it run
down flowers, arms, feet.
No longer.
May's welcome gift
is September's cruel encouragement.

Yesterday I signed the hospital forms
to remove my father's feeding tube.

One Almost Cleared the Pasture Fence

Creative Nonfiction Winner

• Mim Kagol

Picture a house in the country, a fifties rambler, not a farmhouse. But no anachronism; it fits there, it looks right. The house is barn-red; there is a brick planter along the front and a huge elm tree out by the mailbox. Inside the house, one entire wall of the huge living room is books, floor to ceiling. Guests comment on that ("Oh, my, so many books!") even before they remark on the view from the picture window ("What a magnificent view!"). The woman of the house always says, modest and thoughtful, "Well, we like it."

Put her back outside in the yard: A woman about thirty-seven years old, sleeveless blouse, everyday shorts. Her feet in their old tennis shoes hurt her, always, but she has garden dirt on her hands, and she is happy. Flowers and books and family. All this. She is a college teacher and has a reputation in the community for grace and intellect. She is well-spoken. Someday she may write all her life's stories, but not show them to her mother.

Her family: A husband, he does very well in sales and is a weekend farmer here where they live on forty acres. Two miles west of North Mankato, at the southernmost point of Nicollet County, just where the Minnesota River makes a V and heads north. You've seen it on maps. Their three children: a boy and two girls. (Another girl, a late surprise, will come in about seven years.) The children are sun-browned and normal. The woman loves and admires them.

She walks the perimeter of her yard, tallying with growing annoyance all the spots where the horses have stretched their liquid necks over the chain-link fence and eaten the prettiest phlox—the pinks and purples, never the plain white ones—and the delphiniums. "Ray!" she calls, hands on her hips. Something must be done about this.

But he is in the pasture playing ball with their kids and a few more from the neighborhood. She opens the gate to the pasture and goes to wait and watch. Look at those children—so agile and complete! (She has given them everything she longed for in childhood: horses, a dog, roller skates, swimming lessons, new back-to-school clothes every fall, plaid book satchels with buckles and a handle, and plenty of tablets for writing and math. The Depression, her children know, was harsh in a special way to the six children of a Lutheran minister in the parched and windblown Red River Valley.)

She watches her kids, how they casually smack the ball, no matter what the pitch. High, outside, low and inside, they can hit anything their dad puts in front of them. They will never know what it was like to be chosen last in recess games. Or not even chosen, just added because left over. The time-honored, callous caste system of the schoolyard exalted broad-shouldered athletes, thick as mules, far above the scholarly giants of the classroom who suffered fallen arches from too-small, hand-me-down shoes. (She who never once in elementary and secondary school misspelled a word.)

She leans against the side of the corncrib that is serving as a backstop. Meaning: no catcher needed. Another reason the children are such good hitters: A strike means you have to retrieve the ball yourself, get it before it rolls under the building or over the hill.

Suddenly surprising herself: "I believe I'll try that, please." Well, all right, then. The youngest is appointed catcher (it will save a great deal of time) and shows her where to stand: the plate. She swings the bat awkwardly, misses five easy ones. In the outfield, the children sigh cruelly.

"Look, Florence," her husband finally says. "Keep your eye on the ball. Watch it all the way. When it gets to you, swing. Put the bat where the ball is." He corrects her grip a little, then strides back to the small rock that marks the pitcher's mound. He sends her a nice, slow, fat one. She watches it all the way, leans back a bit on her right heel, and swings. Oh, my, it feels good. It goes *thwok!* off the end of the bat, a pretty decent line drive that catches her son napping out by second. She shouts, "My hands are tingling!" Her husband grins.

Now the fielders awaken. No base-running, just hits, and she's putting them out there. *Thwok!* Down the first-base line. Another one—*thwok!* —to short. One sizzler almost clears the fence. (A few feet more, over the road and into the soybeans, would be a home run.) *Thwok!* Why didn't anyone ever tell her this before: "Keep your eye on the ball"? This is so beautiful; it explains so much.

Thwok! She won't quit. "Okay, Mom," the kids yell. "Time's up. Give us our turn." No! She won't. Every pop fly, every line drive, every grounder through the infield awes into rueful silence those swaggering farm boys who couldn't spell John Deere, those saucy town girls who thought Macbeth was a girl, every River Valley Junior High student who wouldn't know a predicate if it reared up off the page and bit their pencil. They ring the pasture, ghostly, watching. And they're impressed. ("Lookin' good . . . Lookin' real good . . . I'll take Florence.")

3

Thwok! Twilight, and the fielders mutiny one by one, citing the "game called on accounta darkness" rule. "Ray!" she declares. "We need (swing—grunt—*thwok!*—) *lights* out here!"

Can you see why, later, in bed, she cannot sleep? Why, when she hears the horses' halters clink against the fence, as their gifted lips select the best blossoms, she doesn't even mind? Tense and electric in her arms and hips is the memory of bat connecting with ball, as pure as the *thwok!* of subject-verb agreement. The joy of of learning, of knowing how, of getting it right.

She is vindicated.

She is redeemed.

She is, understandably, awake for a long time.

Walking the Line

Fiction Winner • Cheyenne Marco

Katie headed south out of her backyard, toward the Federated Co-op. She walked down the pitted sidewalk of Main Street and past the empty, haunted storefronts. Nobody her age could remember there ever being anything in them but cobwebs and Friday night rendezvous. She and the twenty-four other seniors at Minnow Creek High—her entire graduating class —could jimmy those locks so no one would know. But everyone knew in this town, not because there were eyes everywhere but because her parents had gotten in the same kind of trouble and her grandparents and her great-grandparents.

The Co-op stood in the center of town, an inconvenience for everyone. In the fall, grain carts and semis clogged the streets. The corn dryers deafened the whole town and covered them with a blanket of corn dust. But Katie loved the Co-op in the spring, because it brought the trains straight through the heart of town. Something about the keening of the train whistle sounded like music as it arched over octaves and resounded through the town. When the wheels sent metallic screams through the Midwestern air, it was the only time this place felt full, like there was something here besides corn and camo and booze. It was the only time she felt there was movement.

When she reached the Co-op, she ducked around the elevator and found the tracks. They crisscrossed here, some passing under the grain spout and others circumventing the whole setup. But they all converged and stretched east and west. She looked at the steel and timbers and began to follow them west.

She always walked the tracks when she needed to think. She mounted the rail, walking the thin line like a tightrope walker. Her ankles threatened to give way, wobbling under her careful steps. She took a breath and kept walking. The sun glinting off the metal hurt her eyes, but she dared not close them. Every time she did, she saw the same thing: her clothes falling away, Zach's sure hands on her hips, his lips against her neck. It had been a pleasant image for weeks, and she held onto the details like he had held her—firmly, tenderly, passionately. No one could be so much in love; no one could cherish their first time as much as she had. As such, she repeated it as often as they could: in his truck, at the lake, behind the school. And like the first, she held onto these moments as well, calling them to memory with fondness and a flush she could feel all the way to her toes.

Until the strip turned pink.

It was as if that tiny piece of plastic absorbed every blush, every drop of blood from her missed period until it screamed with the definitiveness that now seemed to define her life.

She knew what her father would say. Nothing. Her mother would cry but cherish digging out the old baby crib—the solid oak basket that had been passed down from her mother's mother. Her friends would shrug. Happens all the time. Glad it's not me. The town would talk. Poor Katie. The least likely! That's what you get.

It all unfolded in her head. Her pregnant belly would swell like her mother's had. She would live in a house like her grandmother's. She'd raise her family like her great-grandmother had. It'd be the same story in the same town. A hundred years on repeat. Her parents would help. She and Zach would get married, probably after the baby so she could fit into her mother's wedding dress. They'd live here the rest of their lives. She'd work at the Pit Stop, spend her afternoons gossiping with Ellen and washing corn dust out of bed linens. Zach would work at the elevator and drink Windsor down at the Trading Post. The kid, eventually kids, would run around in the front yard and stain the bottoms of their feet green and brown, christened by the Minnesota earth.

It was a track, a straight path that she would never be able to jump —a path as determined and limitless as the one she walked.

She didn't want to be a mother. One day. After she'd gone to college, swum off the shore of Australia, learned to play the guitar, moved to Minneapolis (the perfect combination of close and far enough). One day but not today. And she loved Zach, maybe enough to marry someday. Someday but not today and not here.

But she couldn't *not* be a mother. The mere thought conjured screaming. Her father would turn her out. Her mother would forbid it. Her grandparents would lecture her about hell. Zach would protest, and his parents would find some way to stop her. And she couldn't do the procedure secretly. There were no secrets in this goddamned town.

She was having a baby.

So she spent the last week agonizing over the mental images and feeling everything shrink as her body imperceptibly expanded. She imagined gaudy maternity shirts, the pale yellow of her would-be kitchen, the long years of walking past empty storefronts.

A breeze carried the scent of hog manure. Gary Turner was preparing for the spring plant. If she closed her eyes, she could see him in the field, spreading the fertilizer. She hated that she knew the smell and whose field it came from. The landscape around her morphed into fields only infrequently interrupted by trees. The tree branches reached upward like arthritic fingers. Buds started to bloom into new leaves. Katie admired the sharp line where the earth met the sky. There was beauty out here. She couldn't deny that. It became more beautiful the farther she walked from town. She wanted to walk forever.

She tried thinking of other things, but eventually her mind became empty. She watched the Canadian geese fly overhead. She listened to their chatter. The sun rested on her cheekbones. The warmth reminded her of Zach and, for a moment, she recaptured the ecstasy of his touch and the happiness she'd felt. Maybe it would be okay.

Her serenity was interrupted by a train whistle. She stayed on the tracks. It was miles behind her. She pictured the spray-paint on the rusty cars. Gang tags and pudgy caricatures that originated from Detroit or Chicago, places she'd never been and would probably never go. She decided in that moment, if she hadn't gotten pregnant, she'd have been a train conductor. She'd have moved back and forth between the coasts, moving with the speed and force that only a train could generate.

She sighed. As soon as possible, she'd tell Zach. They could decide what they wanted from each other. Maybe he'd propose; that'd soften the blow when they told their parents. Her heart leapt as the train whistle sounded again. She couldn't be a train conductor. She was never good at staying on the same path. It was boring. It'd be the same landscape over and over again. Sure, it'd be exciting the first time, but it would eventually get stale. The same mountains and rivers, the same twists and turns. The whistle blasted again, and she could hear the creak of the wheels on the rail.

She stepped to the side. The gravel crunched beneath her feet.

If she hadn't gotten pregnant, she would have been a landscape architect. She looked at the wide, empty land before her, and she thought how she would've loved spending her life filling it. But she'd gotten off track. She wouldn't be a landscape architect. There was no fixing that.

She stepped onto the tracks, then off again. On and off. On and off. She created a dance.

The music of the train grew louder, and she imagined the beauty of it, the force of it as it drove forward. She felt everything moving forward so quickly that she couldn't wrap her head around it. Everything lurched forward —everything but her. Life moved her backwards or maybe she had moved herself backwards.

She smiled and stepped back onto the tracks.

Sunday Afternoon at the
Auction Barn

Poetry 2nd Place

• Audrey Kletscher Helbling

Shoulder brushes shoulder as bidders settle onto plank benches
in the tightness of the arched roof auction barn,
oil stains shadowing the cement beneath their soles,
where a farmer once greased wheel bearings on his Case tractor.

The auctioneer chants in a steady cadence
that mesmerizes, sways the faithful fellowship
to raise hands, nod heads, tip bidding cards
in reverent respect of an aged rural liturgy.

Red Wing crock, cane back rocker, a Jacob's Ladder quilt,
Aunt Mary's treasured steamer trunk, weathered oars—
goods of yesteryear coveted by those who commune here,
sipping steaming black coffee from Styrofoam cups.

Skating the Edge of Memory

Creative Nonfiction 2nd Place

• Charmaine Pappas Donovan

Certain experiences flit about like mosquitoes at screen doors on dark nights—like the time Mother caught a firefly in her freckled hands, then released its blinking body back into darkness. If I were bright enough, if my bulb shined incandescent, I could pour light into murky corners. I would query full moons. Perhaps the sting of recollection would extract from me the blood, the essence of those memories, and I could find a bigger part of who I am, and am becoming, by turning over time the way I've dug for worms in deep soil.

I can't remember the smell of my mother, her unwashed body-closeness, the odor of coffee with cream on her breath. Once more I wish to find her wearing her pea-green apron trimmed in rick-rack and dusted by flour, leaning on a rolling pin as she flattens pie dough. I can't even remember who I was before language lit a fire in my mind and its smoke became a screen through which I viewed everything. I don't recollect the wrinkled face of Mrs. Street, my first grade teacher, who introduced me to words. She made our class wear paper towel slippers stapled together. Slippers we skated across waxed floors, ones we wore on spring days when shoes were too muddy for the classroom.

If only I could remember the joy in swinging—how my weight glided through space and sky on a sunny day. I took no notice of my underpants, bright as dandelions, flashing beneath my dress. My legs pumped forward and back, forward and back.

I don't know why I strain to remember intermittent images igniting my brain, fireflies in dusky meadows. Why do I recall things better forgotten: dead coyotes, flat and scuzzy, in Mr. Busse's refuse pile circled by rot-smell and green-bodied flies? Why can I not remember why I went downstairs, but must return to the kitchen to find the image of bread in the basement freezer? I wish I could remember the last lunch with Mom before her cancer diagnosis, how we huddled over our rice pudding savoring plump raisins and the familiar tang of cinnamon, that day when I still believed she might live forever.

Those Long Winter Mornings

Fiction 2nd Place • Chet Corey

She'd fed him hot oatmeal winter morning after long winter morning for forty-eight years. Their breakfast table had been a three-by-two-foot table braced against one wall of the kitchen for thirty of those forty-eight. Before that, it had been his mother's in the old farm place—a utility table, good for whatever put to use. It cornered the outside wall with its east-facing window, like a third at table—an uninvited, morning guest.

She pulled the window curtain with its wintery landscape along the bronze-colored rod, as she had with each change of season. For years, always the same curtain for that season. But she'd been late this year and only the week before had folded away the curtain with its blaze of Sugar Maple leaves and hung the wintery landscape.

Alvin had died in late fall. And yet she'd sat with him at that kitchen table into late winter, Alvin's ashes filling three-quarters to the top of the cardboard mortuary's container, so like old Quaker Oats boxes she'd emptied over forty-eight years. But Alvin's ashes, she had not. Nor would she empty them out—scatter him across the garden come spring. She had him where she'd wanted him, and Alvin would have to sit and listen, whether she gossiped, cursed him out over some old neglect, or talked the long morning over the telephone with Edith.

That, Alvin, is what comes with cremation, she reminded him. Too cheap to buy them both a burial plot, too lazy to scrape and repaint the kitchen wall and window casings. Too lazy to fix the window's warp so she could open it more than two inches in the summer's heat. Too quick to get up before she'd finished—or even started *her* own oatmeal.

The fault was partly his mother's. She admitted that. Alvin's mother having fed the hired hands and threshers—besides the family—before she'd serve herself on their old farm place. And, like Alvin, his father would be done and up before Alvin's mother sat down. His chair, like Alvin's, never put right. Alvin would be up quick as it took him to eat the bowl of three-minute oatmeal she'd set before him.

But he'd been slow with the blue paint for that kitchen wall—half those thirty years too slow. Fifteen years she'd waited for him to repaint that wall. And so he'd have to sit and wait while she finished her bacon and jellied toast and eggs and talked on and on about whatever he'd say was "a bunch of hooey." And she'd hated oatmeal. Wasn't going to waste another three minutes to make it ever again. She'd bought her own plot, too, with some of that life insurance. Let his in-laws—any of them that'd be left after she'd be gone and in the ground—decide about his ashes.

She had Edith to ring up for their morning talk about planting gladiola bulbs from the spring catalogue. And Alvin could sit and listen, just where she'd set him, quiet as paint dries.

Aria

Poetry • Tim J Brennan

When the fat lady sings
and it's time, I would like music
to murder me—
something elegant like Chopin—

I wouldn't want people at my funeral
humming, or worse, tapping scuffed shoes
to any old wordless tune

I'd rather die with a song in my head:
something with violins, like cricket legs
softly rubbing on the first frost
of October, a white-haired preacher
with a thin baton, and Jesus Christ
at the backdoor, making sure no one
leaves without tipping the collection

Parade

Poetry • Lina Belar

Over the lake
the wind strides
dragging his great
purple cape, rippling
the water. On the shoreline
grasses bow in homage while
trees in the forest wave
and wave and
wave.

Comfort

I grab my bag and step out the screen door while the siren screams. The rain soaks my dress before my sister can exit as well. Working two summers here means I know that the screen door always slams. This time I can't hear it shut amid the straight rain, rumbling air, and Sauk Centre's shrieking town siren.

The key ring I hold has three keys. I don't know which one opens the padlock, but I know one does. My flip-flops slap the wheelchair ramp.

Does the siren mean a tornado touched down or that there's just a serious threat?

I can't remember which it is, but I know we need to enter the cellar. My hand slips along the paint-peeling handrail and I whip around the end so I stand at the cellar doors. My sandals sink two-inches deep in the puddle that pooled in the minute or two since the rain began. I squat and grab the padlock. The chains likely rattle as usual, but the only sound my ears notice is that siren telling me we're not safe where we are.

I search the keys, hoping one is labeled "Master" like the lock. I find none, so I jam the first silver key into the keyhole. My hand shakes the lock and chain as I wrench the key. It doesn't turn. I regret not unlocking this earlier when the clouds first accumulated.

I switch keys, a gold one this time. This key won't even enter the lock. A curse word traverses my mind, but my mouth yells, "Go knock on a door!" I don't even look at her, but whom else could I be commanding? Every other person is hidden away indoors.

"Which one?" Becky asks me. I start working with the other silver key, the last key.

"ANY ONE!" It's not frustration making me yell; I need her to hear me the first time, so we don't waste precious minutes repeating ourselves.

This key does nothing either. I don't watch which way Becky goes, but I know she leaves. Adrenaline and the cold rain create shivers, and the keys shake.

I try the first key again.

The sky sounds like a train. The sky sounds like a train. Train equals tornado. Oh, God . . .

The key won't turn and I quit trying. I stand and look behind me. By now, Becky must have found a willing neighbor. I can't see her though. I run to the front yard, looking through two rain layers—the one coating my glasses and the one falling.

To the left is the creepy old man's house. He wears open-collared Hawaiian shirts and a gold chain. He weeds his flowerbeds and smokes a cigarette, while leering down the street. I hope she didn't choose his door. His porch is empty, so I look across the street. I don't see her there either.

I scream her name, but she won't hear me no matter how I yell.

My adrenaline-high mind creates an image—a tornado, my sister, and explaining to my mom what the hell we were doing outside.

I slosh back again. There. I see her on the elderly couple's back stoop. The lilac bush blocked my view earlier, but this new angle means I see her orange dress.

I arrive just as she calls, "Can we come in your basement?"

"Yes, yes. Come in," says a voice.

We enter and shed our flip-flops, not that our feet are much cleaner or drier. Twelve quick steps and we reach their carpeted basement that smells like our great-grandparents' house. The old television set shows the weather channel, the whole screen tinted yellow-green. The woman covers my sister and me with brown and orange afghans, saying we must be cold.

The Gift

Poetry Honorable Mention

• Janice Larson Braun

My daughter's gaze
Finds me across the room
As Christmas presents explode
All around us,
Wrapping paper drifting down,
Slowly covering the floor.
As the love from her smile
Melts into my pores,
All the shouts and giggles
Of generations
Simply disappear.
I feel the warmth traveling
Up my bones and into my chest—coalescing there
Where it circles a few times
Before lying down, content,
Where I will be able to hold it
In the certain cold months ahead,
Long after some plane
Takes her away.

Pink Striped Language

Poetry • Doris Lueth Stengel

I'm hanging your sheets on the line today, Mama. The same sheets you hung on your clothesline fifty years ago. The pink striped ones, not as bright as they were then. These were your best sheets, the ones you used when visitors came. This cotton coarser and stiffer than today's high thread count and blends, but durable.

>whipped by prairie wind
>Monday morning statement
>housewife on duty

When I came home from college these sheets welcomed me with perfume of April's sweet hope. This fragrance assured me that I was loved even though I cannot remember you voicing that. Our house quiet with German understatement. No talk of sheets or beds or sex.

>few words, few touches
>quick stiff hugs, hello goodbye
>talcum-scented caring

In early years of our marriage we came home with three babies in tow. We slept on your pink stripes. You spoke of mundane things, the garden, the green beans. Daddy talked less—the weather, the crops, the store. We knew your heart was damaged by childhood illness but we did not know how soon that heart would stop. And break ours.

>pink stripes on the line
>flag from a silent country
>surrendered to death

Proper Names

Creative Nonfiction

• Lynne Maker Kuechle

Shakespeare said it—if not first, then memorably. What's in a name? Perhaps mere coincidence glazed the word *rose* with the texture of a petal. Or centuries of association turned four slurry letters into a metaphor for beauty. Even so, it's difficult to imagine a *prickleweed* or *glund* smelling as sweet.

Names matter.

We label things—and people—to lay claim to them, to describe them, to keep track of them, to love them. Perhaps the Russians do it best: altering names to signify relationships, using diminutives that often—paradoxically—lengthen and stretch, rolling slowly off the tongue to denote deepening levels of sweetness, tenderness. Aleksander might be your co-worker; Sasha your brother, Sashenka your boyfriend, Sashunya your child. One person, four levels of intimacy. As the consonants grow softer, the vowels bulge. The link between speaker and named becomes obvious to anyone within earshot.

I've never been fond of my name, the one my mother chose specifically because it resisted a nickname. Because she, Jeannette, hated being reduced to Netsie, I grew up saddled with a one-syllable, unisex appellation. As Lynn Swann gained fame with the Pittsburgh Steelers, I began looping an "e" onto the name we shared, hoping it would curtail the junk mail that came addressed to "Mr."

I longed to complete my signature by frosting a heart over an "i," as Cyndi, Patti and Lori could. At the very least, I coveted a designation that people could truncate intimately—something like Kath, Ter, Mare. Something to show that they knew me well, had permission to change my name, held claim to at least one version of me: a public declaration that I mattered.

Such one-syllable utterances aren't soft and flowing like Russian diminutives, but they serve the same purpose: erecting boundaries, like an inside joke; placing *you and me* within our sphere, keeping others out. And although many American nicknames are terse, they overcome the short, harsh sound because of the understanding that more letters exist, the name is longer, but because of our closeness those excess syllables are unnecessary. None of those connotations are possible with my name. Shrinking Lynne—to what, Luh? —would be like tripping on a rug, splattering sauce on a silk blouse.

For many years, I had a similar dislike for my last name: Maker, a simple Anglo-Saxon noun that people regularly mispronounce Maher, Macker or Marker. Throughout grade school, I was asked, "Hey, Maker, what d'ya make?"

A friend's brother called me May-cow and mooed at me in the halls. I blamed my parents. Didn't they realize I was born to be Rebecca McCallister or Elizabeth Worthington, a multi-syllable concoction of pitches that rise and fall, curves that bend and beckon like a dancer?

Not until I was out of school did I meet an artist who honored my name. We worked together, in the days before Word and Pagemaker, proofreading galleys, cutting out text and photos, and pasting them onto pages that would become the company magazine. On layout days, there was plenty of time to converse. One day Berta brought me a neatly typed definition that I've saved all these years: *maker; synonyms poet, creator, author; suggestive of using material as an instrument through which one gives form to one's ideas.* "It's the perfect name for a writer!" she gushed. "And capitalized, you know, 'Maker' designates God."

My birth name meant God. When kids asked me what I made, I should have said *art*. Or maybe: *everything.*

So perhaps I erred when I added my husband's German surname to my string of monikers. Obviously, it's even less likely than *Maker* to be pronounced correctly; numerous attempts have resulted in Kook-lee, Koo-shell, Koo-chell-ee and, twice, by the same telemarketer: Key-knuckle. (In fact it's Keek-lee, rhymes with *weekly,* although my husband's father coughed out a guttural *Kek-hlee* that his non-German-speaking descendants can't replicate.)

My new last name translates into *little cake.* It does not liken me to the Almighty.

I named my dolls, my dogs, stuffed animals, characters in the stories I wrote. I gave nicknames to friends, family, the man who became my husband. But when we adopted our Russian daughter, we had only minimal input into what we would call her.

Watching the videotape that introduced us, we needed several viewings before we deciphered the sounds that turned Victoriya into Vica, a name that made her smile. When we carried her home, she brought just one thing: that first name, bestowed by a vanished birth mother to honor a ghostly birth father.

We learned the first diminutive, but not the subsequent ones, the longer, softer ones. The ones that say publicly what we nonetheless feel: *You are the closest thing in the world to me. Closer than the length of an umbilical cord.*

Sorting

Poetry • Marilyn Wolff

When Dad died, not much changed around that house.
But when Mother died, we sorted through their things—
our baby clothes in the attic, now sixty years old,
Dad's Army uniform, thick with dust,
picture albums we had never seen,
unrecognizable canned goods in the basement,
our favorite dolls still in the closet, unseeing eyes wide open,
half-naked and untouched for years,
boxes of buttons and zippers, still waiting to be used,
half-finished quilts, long forgotten.
Scraps of fabric brought memories of school dresses
and summer shirts.
Give that away—throw those away—
must keep these—maybe we can sell that.
We rushed through the piles—
rifling through their lives,
sorting through our grief.

The Sunbathers

Poetry • Laura K Murray

Held in place by side rails and sedatives
he lies under feeble lights, displayed
in a crinkle cut gown for us prayerful
few and a nurse with dry knuckles. His
breaths scrape in and out, in in   and out
Waiting—

It's up to him now, this holding on
or letting go, I'm not sure which.
His chin and chest and brows strain
upward as if inviting the burn of
invisible rays, and I remember

the kiddie-corner neighbor girl
who woke up without a mother
and refused to eat anything all summer
besides graham crackers and
dented backyard plums,

who parked belly button up
on her daddy's station wagon
roof, rolling-pin limbs dark
and slippery with Johnson's
baby oil. I watched with telescope

pupils and air-conditioned interest
as she sucked on plum pits
squeezed sweat from her eyes
grasped at the heat steaming
thicker in in   and out her lungs
Waiting—

Waiting

He's late. She stands by the kitchen sink and stares out the window, longing for his headlights to flood the deserted street. She looks at her watch again: 7:14. Where is he? He knows tonight marks their one year anniversary when they first met. Though he hadn't picked up his phone at the office, she'd left a voice mail with a perky reminder that she was preparing a special dinner tonight, so why is he over an hour late?

She checks her watch again: 7:22. Usually she doesn't mind the long hours he spends at the office because then she knows where he is, but he's never been this late. No doubt, a long-winded client is the reason why he hasn't called.

Watching her blurry reflection in the window, her kohl-rimmed eyes look sunken and hollow in the darkening shadows. A long-lost childhood memory resurfaces, a haunted, lonely image of her mother standing by a window, waiting for her father to come home. She grimaces, feeling weak and slightly nauseous, and tries to convince herself she isn't walking in her mother's shoes.

Behind her the table is set for two with her good dishes. Polished wine glasses dance with the flickering flames from twin candles. On the kitchen counter, a vase waits to quench the thirst of a dozen red roses. Dinner warms in the oven and its rich aroma will greet him at the door, enticing him to drop to his knees tonight. Andrea Bocelli croons a love song in the background and, for a moment, her eyes slip closed in ecstasy.

In her dream-like euphoria, the waiting is torture, yet alluring, like teetering on the edge of a volcanic eruption. She's in love with him. She fought it at first, because her previous lovers were unfaithful men who used her when they knew she loved them. So she has kept her love for him to herself, but she has bound him to her so he can't get away. On this memorable night, she'll surprise with those three special words. And later, when the time is right, she'll share a secret she's been waiting to tell him.

She wears the little red dress he bought her after their third date. Now it hugs her body like a glove. The thin straps dig into her shoulders, and the plunging neckline, that once was suggestive, extravagantly exposes her blossoming figure. She sucks in her belly and tugs the fabric over her hips.

Her skin glows after soaking in a tub of bubbles. The lingering scent swirls around her, seductive and hypnotic. Her hair is a tangle of curls, sexy and wild, just the way he likes it. Her nails match her dress, fiery red pearls that, later, will dance over his skin.

He's never late. She hides her impatience as she refolds the napkins and straightens the silverware. She sets the wine corkscrew next to the vase and wipes invisible dust from the counter. She meets her gaze in the bathroom mirror, smiles slightly at her midsection, and decides that she looks pretty—although anyone would look pretty in the soft lighting. Like her mother, she doesn't believe in fluorescent lighting.

Worry creases her forehead and for the last time, she promises herself, she checks her watch: 8:38. She paces the floor and retraces her footsteps to the window. Still no car. Damn him for making her feel this way. She curses him and curses herself for caring so much and being so careless with her love.

The excitement of a romantic evening fizzles with each passing minute. Her toes pinch in her stilettos. Lavish Beef Wellington shrivels inside its crumbling puff pastry, like a cheap hotdog left on a picnic table in the hot sun. Its juice evaporates, waiting too long for a splash of red wine to drizzle over her work of art. The candles drown in their own wax and the smoldering wicks wave smoke signals.

She weighs the risks of being clingy and not knowing if he's been in an accident, or something worse, and decides to call his cell phone. The phone rings and rings, her heart racing with something close to fear. Finally he answers softly as if he's whispering. In the background children's screams and laughter shout out like gunfire.

"Where are you? Dinner was ready hours ago," she asks, tucking her hand under her perspiring arm. Feeling desperate for some sort of clue, she asks as breezily as possible, "Whose kids are with you?"

His silence stretches like a taut rubber band and then snaps her heart when she overhears an unfamiliar woman's voice ask him, "Who is it?" His voice is flippant when he says, "Just a wrong number." Click. The snap of his phone slaps her in the face. In stunned disbelief, her jaw drops and shock sucks the air from her lungs. Her head buzzes and the drone of the dial tone finally speaks to her—the waiting is over.

Moving as if in a daze, she opens the bedroom door. Her wrinkled dress falls to the floor in a puddle. She kicks off her high heels and they flop on their sides as if they had broken ankles. She climbs into bed, turns away from his pillow and faces the window. She stares long and hard, connecting the dots of the stars. The crescent moon taunts her with a lopsided grin, and she feels like a lone fool in the universe.

She's alone, yet not alone. She pulls her mother's quilt under her chin and rests her hands on her stomach, on the life growing inside her. Hot tears cling to the corners of her eyes while Bocelli sings the last stanza of his lovesick hit, "It's Time to Say Goodbye," and then she finally cries.

Tornado

Poetry • Lina Belar

After the June rains, we returned
to our tumbled town and heard
the story a hundred times that day
on the news, in the cafe.

In some neighborhoods
the damage seems random,
a roof here, a wall there,
a whole garage uprooted,
replanted a block away.

In the countryside, they say,
cows hang in trees with pieces
of tin from metal buildings
that looked like kites
sailing on an unholy wind.

Here at the center there is nothing
undamaged, unturned, unskewed.
Trees are uprooted, cemetery stones
tossed about like children's blocks,
delphiniums lay strewn about the garden paths
like sentries caught off guard.

No lives were lost, thank God,
though one man's heart gave out later
as he surveyed the broken town.
Like war, everyone dies a little bit.
No one talks about it anymore.

Fog

Poetry • Jeanne Emrich

Above the slumbering marsh,
I hear the rip-song of wings.
The air is the color of blue milk,
visibility is zero—and still, they come.
They will rest and yet not rest.
Every moment is a possibility.
There will be false starts,
there will be trial runs,
until at last the time will come
when they will lift and wheel
toward the one direction,
the one truth that is sure.
Even in fog, the wild geese
know the way south.
For that kind of certainty,
I would risk a short life.

Minnesota Smoke

Creative Nonfiction Honorable Mention

• Cheyenne Marco

My hair smells like wood smoke and diesel. The cool night air nips at my ears and fingertips. The flames shimmy and writhe in the pit; they cast shadows that flicker against the trees and campers.

I lean into my lawn chair and continue my argument with Matt. We bicker about the best version of "Hallelujah." I say it's Wainwright while he contends it's Buckley. Two years later, when he drives down to congratulate me on passing my comprehensive exams, we have the same argument. Matt is the most passionate man I know. He loves, hates, and learns with a kind of intensity reserved for movies. He's the hero in the romantic comedy, the sweet nerd who morphs into the superhero.

Arnie sits in the next chair. He's a bawdy man with my sense of humor. He's got a porn 'stache and a laugh more unique than Fran Drescher's. He tells me stories about college, when he and his friends were visited by the cops and instead of quieting down offered to pay the noise violation so they could keep on partying. He tells me he vowed to never propose to a woman, only to end up drunk and down on one knee. He named his snowmobile "Amy" and his golf cart "Meriwether." He's too eccentric to be real.

There's Chuck who drives with his knee on icy roads, Ed who rebuilt a motorcycle, Noah who skis behind duck boats, and Aaron who inadvertently created a hostage situation. These men are all related or work together, and they camp just south of me. I've lost count of how many of them there are. When I started camping next to them, I avoided them simply because they outnumbered me so badly. Once, for the Fourth of July holiday, I texted my best friend and told her there weren't that many people at Woodstock. Mainly, large families made no sense to me, because I'd never had any experience with them My childhood had not been filled with grandparents, cousins, or uncles, and from what I'd gathered from Clark Griswald movies, I wasn't missing much.

However, the neighbors' laughter drifted over to my side of the fence, and I laughed with them, without cause. Arnie fished me out of my solitude. As a writer, a nerd, and an anti-socialite (or whatever excuse I was using back then), I cherished my isolation, but the neighbors recruited me for drunken lake games and fireside chats. In the daylight, they slingshot rubber chickens into laundry baskets. At night, they quizzed me on what I wanted from life and what were the things in life I regretted. When they detected my introversion, Arnie's goal became to loosen me up, to give me a drink, to get me to do something stupid. I might not have been making memories at college, but he was determined I would make them around this fire. At the very least, I would laugh.

And I did.

I laughed a lot.

I wouldn't categorize myself as a girly-girl, and I wouldn't go so far as to call myself a tomboy. I wear pink camo. I drive a truck with cutesy seat covers. I walk that line. I grew up with brothers, which meant I became fluent in hunting and farming. In social situations, I found I could more easily converse about pheasant populations than I could about who wore what where. Guy-speak seemed simpler to me. Less pretense. If you thought someone was a bastard, you told him; you didn't befriend him and spread rumors when his back was turned—at least that's how it seemed to me in my juvenile estimation. So, I fell in with the guys. This pattern continued: Matt and John in high school, Josh in college, Austin and Wes in grad school. Friends. Nothing more.

It seemed natural for me to fall in with the campfire crew, the late-night circle of men around a Minnesota fire. The love of the lake ran deep, and they had the same fondness for sex jokes and political debates that I did. As we sat around the fire, telling stories about snowmobiling in Wyoming and cussing out professors, there was no pretense. I could be me. I could be happy.

One day, while shopping with my mom, I told her about my friends.

"You shouldn't hang out with all those guys," she said. "You'll get a reputation."

A reputation.

She explained it to me. Women who hung out with men were dangerous, less-than-women. They stole husbands; they lost their femininity while using it to the extreme.

I felt crushed.

In high school, one of my friends was a guy who liked to hang out with the girls. Even though he dated, there were constant rumors that he was gay; he spent a lot of time struggling with the stigma. I always felt bad for him. Now I knew how he felt. Life had reduced us in very similar ways.

Two years after this incident with my mom, I used it as an example in my Introduction to Literature course to teach gender criticism. Guys who hang out with girls are "fags." Girls who hang out with guys are "sluts."

After a few weeks of hanging out, Arnie shows up at my door with an oversized thermos.

"If you're going to be one of us, you have to have a Bubba Keg," he says, handing over the thermos.

I hold it in my hands, admiring the jade etching. A lump builds in my throat as I contemplate the meaning of "us." In the past few days, I've been referred to as an "adopted family member" and "one of the guys." I'm officially accepted, an established regular.

Holding the glass, I think about my mom and how she would disapprove. I smile. I'm happy to be one of the guys. I thank Arnie for the glass.

They say blood is thicker than water, but nothing is thicker than Minnesota smoke.

Depths

Poetry • Susan Niemela Vollmer

The strident voice of my elementary swim teacher
Belittled our quivering fears and pleading protests
As she lined us up to jump off the diving board

The skilled swimmers at the front of the line
Dove in cleanly or jumped briskly
Laughed as their heads rose sleekly to the surface

Inched out on the board, I fell more than jumped
Struggled through turquoise, ultramarine, indigo
Until an impatient arm dragged me back to breath

Josephine

Fiction Honorable Mention

• Paisley Kauffmann

The screen door slammed. Josephine jumped and smudged her freshly painted toes.

"Damn it."

Baby Harry started to cry.

"Double-damn it."

"Sorry," Harold Jr. said.

"He was sleeping."

"He can't sleep all the time. You need to interact with him more. Try a game."

"Is that what your mama said? Well, I can't play a game with him, because he can barely hold his head up."

Harold Jr. didn't respond and stood in front of his crying son strapped into his car seat on the porch.

"Since you woke him, you can quiet him down," Josephine said, applying polish over the smudge.

"I got to go meet Daddy and I'm running late."

"Well, go," she said from the porch swing. "Don't keep the corn or, God forbid, Big Harold waiting."

Harold Jr. squatted and nudged Baby Harry's belly. "Bye, little buddy. I'll see you tonight."

Stepping towards Josephine, Harold Jr. leaned down to kiss her goodbye and she gave him her cheek. He clomped down the steps in his steel-toed boots and stuck his cowboy hat over his golden locks. The Ford pickup accelerated down the gravel driveway followed by a cloud of dust.

Josephine rocked in the swing watching the warblers busy themselves. The prairie grass swayed in the breeze.

Baby Harry broke Josephine's reverie with a hungry fuss. Checking her polish before she stood, she entered the house and let the screen door slam behind her. Baby Harry howled at her absence.

"Hold on." She pulled a bottle of formula from the fridge. Although her mother-in-law preached its importance, breastfeeding was not for her. Running the bottle under the hot faucet, she thought, *Good enough.*

"Now quit fussing." Josephine held the bottle for him as he smacked. Resting her chin on her hand, she closed her eyes. The din of an approaching car hummed down the highway, but Josephine didn't open her eyes until the gravel crunched. Karen's blue Pinto raced down the driveway toward her. Josephine wanted to check her reflection, but she was trapped with the bottle in her hand.

"Josephine, I've got super news," Karen said, running up the porch stairs. "Hi, Baby Harry. You're so handsome, just like your daddy. You need to get him out of the sun." She took the bottle from Josephine, slid the car seat into the shade, and popped the bottle back in his mouth. "You don't want him to end up with a bunch of freckles, like me, do you?"

"So? What's your super news?" Josephine asked.

"I'm going to Minneapolis."

"For what?"

"I registered at a community college and my dad got me a job at some law office, or accounting office—whatever—as a secretary."

"Wow."

"I'm going to miss you, too." Karen lifted Baby Harry from the car seat and set him in her lap. She patted his back to elicit a burp. "He's soaking wet."

"Is he?"

"I'll change him." Karen hurried inside with Baby Harry. The screen door slammed shut and Josephine flinched. A drop of water landed on her thigh and another. Realizing the drops were tears, she hastily wiped under her eyes.

Karen returned and plopped Baby Harry on her lap. She had dressed him in Garanimals and combed his yellow curls. "Anyways, you won't believe who's coming with me."

"Who?" Josephine's stomach gripped as she was forced to understand two locals were escaping.

"Mary Woodrich. Remember how the poor thing tried out for cheerleading every year? I told her you weren't going to let her make the squad. I mean, seriously, I never even bothered trying out. You probably haven't seen her since graduation, but she's lost twenty pounds and feathered her hair. She's kind of pretty now."

"No way," Josephine said, watching Karen shift Baby Harry from one thigh to the other. Baby Harry's chubby hand reached for Karen's hoop earring, and she playfully waggled her head.

"Mary got into college, real college, at the university. Can you believe it? I always thought she was kind of a weirdo, but I guess she's really smart." Karen struggled to keep a lock of frizzy red hair behind her ear. "Anyways, what have you been doing?"

"Not much," Josephine said, raising her brows at Baby Harry.

"I suppose this guy takes most of your time." Karen squeezed Baby Harry and he drooled on her arm.

"Let me get a rag." Josephine started to get up.

"Don't worry," Karen said, wiping the slobber on her jean shorts. "Remember, I got eight little brothers and sisters. I'm leaving in a few hours, but I just wanted to stop by and say goodbye. I know we haven't talked much since the baby—and I totally understand—I'd be out of touch too. You must be so busy being a new wife and mother."

"Yeah, I guess."

"I'll call you as soon as I'm settled in the big city. I'm so nervous, but excited."

"For sure." Josephine scrutinized her pink-painted toenails.

"Well, I better get going." Karen handed the baby to Josephine, and she set him back in his car seat.

Josephine accepted a quick hug from Karen.

"I'll write and you better write me back," Karen said.

"I will."

Josephine watched Karen's vehicle shrink into the horizon. She walked past the baby, who managed to get his fist into his mouth and cooed contentedly. Josephine's entire being ached with hate. She had never liked Mary Woodrich with her big ass and loud opinions, but today she hated her. What a waste of space in Minneapolis. Standing in the kitchen, she watched the faucet drip into a dirty pot. The impulse to put on make-up distracted her. She would get ready, look pretty, and when Harold Jr. got home she would tell him they were moving to Minneapolis. Harold Jr. wasn't obligated to stay on the farm forever and, with five older brothers, his entitlement was only a sliver of land. Josephine plugged in her curling iron and brushed her long, blond hair. It needed a trim, but she managed to get it feathered.

Smiling at the familiar reflection, she said, "I'm moving to the city. Yes, I'm going alone."

In the mirror, Josephine glimpsed her mother's smug face as history inevitably repeated itself. Her mother had warned her about farm boys' intentions to trap the local girls for wives and mothers in this town. She picked up her curling iron and struck the mirror. It cracked into a spider web pattern distorting her mother's smirk.

Hurrying from the bathroom, she dug her cheerleading duffel bag out of the closet and ran upstairs. She scooped clothes from the dresser and yanked every stitch of clothing from her closet. Breathless, she struggled to zip the bag closed around the tangle of clothes and shoes.

Josephine attempted to lift the bag from the bed, but it was too heavy. She dragged it off the bed and pushed it down the stairs. It rolled down the steps in slow motion and bounced to a stop in front of the screen door. Josephine rushed to the kitchen where a line of nails served as a key rack. Fingering through them, she found the key chain with a silver lightning bolt and ran to the front door. Josephine grasped the handles of the over-sized duffel and pulled it through the screen door, across the porch, and down the steps. The baby pumped his legs and arms, cheering on her effort.

Harold Jr.'s restored 1969 Ford Mustang peeked out from under the dusty car cover. Sprinting towards the prized vehicle with hens scattering and clucking in disapproval, she pulled the car cover off and prayed it would start. Harold Jr. had not paid it any attention since the baby was born. She opened the door and the scent of Armor All reminded her of her lost virginity.

"Come on, please," she whispered, turning the key.

The engine roared to life in its familiar growl and settled into a solid rumble. She rolled toward the front of the house where her large duffel sat expectantly. The baby's mouth puckered in response to the loud automotive that spoke to his future man.

With great effort, Josephine managed to lift the duffel into the trunk. She raced to the driver's seat and bolted down the driveway in a spray of gravel. The sense of freedom, absconding from the life she had unintentionally created, was breathtaking and she gripped the steering wheel to steady her shaking hands. Just before she could turn towards the interstate, her eyes shot to the rearview mirror and her foot stuck to the brake.

She zigzagged backwards towards her son.

Motionless, the baby blinked at her reappearance. She didn't look at his face as she picked up the car seat and carried it inside. She set him on the kitchen table and turned away. The screen door slammed shut and Josephine heard, for the last time, Baby Harry cry for her.

Upper Campground

High above Temperance River,
at the mouth which meets Lake Superior,
the most beautiful, non-reservable campsite
enjoys a vantage point for watching youth
jump from cliffs into the cool water,
beachcombers collect smooth stones,
and vigorous waves crash into basalt boulders.

This idyllic tent site provides a base for
repeated short hikes down to
glacial-formed kettles and
mesmerizing waterfalls,
along volcanic shore,
and hikes back up for refills
of strong camp stove coffee, with
engaging fires that make the evening warm,
and the *coq au vin* in the Dutch oven
burst with amazing and unexpected taste.

Observations

Poetry • Sharon Harris

mirrored in the ruffled river beside me,
horses eating up the sky of clouds—
cantering, churning with long strides,
chewing up their path, the ribbons of color.

my face, my eyes, look back at me—
watch me eat up my future
in great gulps
turning it into my past so fast.

my body, not yet infirm, but not firm either,
can't carry my burdens, real or not—
and my heart—too small to hold
its load of grief.

Screams

Fiction • James Robert Kane

My warfare-obsessed eleven-year-old grandson and I are seated at the kitchen island, paging through his book of military vehicles when he asks, "What was it like in Afghanistan, Grandpa?" and suddenly I see the little girl outside the frost-etched window, staring at me with wide-open, emotionless, haunting eyes.

I see her frequently, almost everywhere I go, in fact, but never before at my grandson's house and instantly I worry that she has intentions upon him as well. I have no weapons that can stop her now. I glance at him quickly to see if he has noticed her, but she is not yet visible to him and, besides, he is busy memorizing tanks. I have told no one about her.

He asks again and I can only offer generalities in words he has already heard: dangerous, traumatic, hot, exhausting, exhilarating. I know what he really wants to understand, but how can I tell him? I cannot even find words for it inside my own mind and fear its true expression will be a volcanic, innards-spewing eruption of a scream that, once released, might never end.

But even if I *could* find words, he is too young, his world too good and full of promise to be prematurely awakened. He still trusts. He still believes. I know that sooner or later he will eat the forbidden fruit, yet right now his innocence is a glorious thing, a shining, protective cloak, and I wish I could touch its hem and be made whole.

I can tell he is impatient with my sanitized answer for he sits drumming his sturdy, athletic fingers on the granite countertop, but there is another hand drumming there, too, skinny with almost translucent skin. He is between her and me, obscuring her except for the hand and the stick-like arm.

"Well, did you kill anyone over there?" he persists, stirring the rumbling magma, and she leans forward to fix those hollow eyes on me, waiting for my answer.

For my scream.

It nearly comes but, quite unexpectedly, he gently slides a hand over mine as he reads my face and says, "It's okay, Grandpa. It's okay."

Almost instantly she vaporizes, and I can almost hear *her* scream. I will hold fast to him for as long as he will permit, for right now he has the greater power. He is my newfound weapon.

The Family Boat

Poetry • Linda Maki

My grandma and grandpa owned a duplex on a
lake in the city. They lived upstairs, my family lived down.
We appeared to be one big happy group, on two floors.

Mornings my grandma greeted me at the top of the
creaky back stairs. Warm toast, dripping butter,
cinnamon smells, and sweet orange juice, just for me.

Afternoons the women restored order to the
communal home, endlessly scrubbing and tidying,
mending and fixing, dusting and fussing.

Dinnertimes my family gathered around
a mahogany table, blue-flowered dishes,
mashed potatoes, roasted meat, pudding.

Bedtimes I soaked long in strawberry
bubbles, then worn flannel PJs and goodnight
kisses from Mom and Gram.

Evening times Grandpa fell down those
now darkened back stairs, cussing.
"Shush"—too many gin and tonics.

Prayer times I would ask God
to make Dad stop yelling, and
slamming doors when he left.

Sleepy times I would wake, scared,
to screaming and shoving against walls
from upstairs or down the hall.

Late at night times I heard the cops
bringing home dear old Dad, Grandpa
or Uncle, while the women scolded.

My family's men, drowning in a whiskey sea.
My family's women, always bailing,
bailing out that two-story boat.

Pinche Migra

Fiction • Patrick Cabello Hansel

I was leaving for school with my violin. It was still winter, but a warm wind had pushed in from the southwest and the big snow pile behind the church had really shrunk. It was barely a mountain anymore, and no one cared about being its king. I had eaten Cocoa Puffs for breakfast, and two sips of my Mami's *cafe*. Dad was doing a double shift at the plant. He'd work for 16 hours, come home, sleep a little, then go back out.

I don't know how the voice pulled me back. I was kicking rocks across the church parking lot where we'd play whiffle ball in the summer, and had just landed one right on second base. The yellow paint of the baselines had gone soft since the fall, and there were puddles. I wanted to be Johan Santana once we started to play again. I wanted to wreck the world with my fastball. I heard the voice; it sounded like my Tio Manuel, so I turned back and the man in the vest motioned me over. Motioned me home.

I was a month from turning six, and this year my birthday was going to fall in Semana Santa. Abuela was already planning the tamales and cake and getting the house ready. My cousin was making her First Holy Communion on Easter too, so it was going to be a whole family celebration. Tios, cousins, my padrinos. Uncle Miguel was going to try to call from Iraq.

Crows were there. *Cuervos.* Big black birds. They had sat on the trees each night for weeks, crying to each other, rising and falling like a giant wave. At night, I would look out my window and see them. Two of them would always break free and sit on the church tower, where the bells were. On Sunday, the old man would turn on the bells and sweep the steps leading up to the big doors. Or if there was snow, he would scrape it off, then pull the bucket of hard salt out and throw it around, like he was feeding chickens. Or pigs. The crows would understand.

I heard the voice, and maybe the voice heard something too. The man had really short hair, but you could see he was *rubio* all the way. Blond and big. He had "ICE" written across his back—hard, like a stop sign. He said, "*Muchacho. Ven aqu,*" but I knew he wasn't speaking in our Spanish. It was loud and choppy and felt like the gun I saw on his hip. He asked me if my mom was home, my dad or Abuela, and since he named almost all the people in our house, I thought he knew me, and knew us. He asked if I could get him a glass of water.

So I opened the door to the kitchen. Mami was still in her bathrobe, feeding Gisela. There was baby oatmeal all over the high chair. Mami's eyes started smiling at me, almost like she knew I was trying to be late for school, and didn't mind. Then her eyes got pointy and dark as the man raised his hands at her. One hand had the badge, the other the gun.

"No pueden entrar en mi casa," she said, slowly, and with the force of wind behind her. *You can't come into my house.* She put her right arm behind the back of the high chair, and motioned me over with her left. I didn't know if I should move or not, if that was what I was supposed to do, and I supposed that that little second of delay is what caused the problem. Mami said, slowly and sharply, like she was hammering some tacks to hold up a curtain: "Omar. Ven aca." *Come here.*

It was a different voice than what I've heard from my mom. Not like when I'm in trouble, exactly, but hard. A little scary. I didn't move at first, and I don't know how long I stood there. Anyway, it doesn't matter, because another man's hand was on my shoulder, gripping hard. I couldn't see him, but I knew he must have been the other guy who came with the *rubio* with the gun. I could smell his neck bending over me, like sweat, like horses and some kind of medicine I had smelled at the hospital.

I should have run to my mom. I should have grabbed onto her, and maybe then the big *guero's* hands, the one with the gun, would not have grabbed her so hard. Mami started screaming and cursing—words that I would never dare use—not around her, or Papi, maybe I would say them when it was just me and my older cousins. But she was calling him "*hijo de puta*" and "*cabron*" and kicking at his hard legs, and trying to hold onto Gisela's high chair, and I couldn't get to her. I couldn't reach across that little kitchen to save my mom, and so when the *guero* with the gun grabbed her hair and pulled her, she was still holding onto the high chair, and it pulled over, all of it, the oatmeal and the sippy cup and my little sister, laughing for some reason, and the whole chair pulled down till my sister hit her head hard on the kitchen table and fell all the way to the floor still strapped in her chair. She cried once, almost like a crow does, sharp and broken in the air, and then she was quiet. Her eyes were open, and they looked at nothing.

My mom was deported, and I didn't see my dad for weeks, until we moved to another house in another part of town. Abuela left back for Mexico soon after. Gisela and I were born here in the U.S., and when my dad couldn't take care of us, we stayed with family, first with Tio Pete and Tia Angela, and then later with Miguel and his girlfriend once he came home from the war. They paid some of Gisela's doctor bills for a while, and then it stopped. She goes to the special part of the school a mile away, limping out to the bus stop with her right leg, the one that doesn't bend like it should. She doesn't talk much, even though she's supposed to be in second or third grade. My aunts and uncles say I don't talk too much anymore, either. I go by the old church in the winter after soccer practice inside the school gym, and I still see the old man tossing salt to the birds.

Sometimes, I think about taking my hand and grabbing onto a crow's back as hard as I can. I want to fly away. I want to strangle that stupid bird.

The Puzzle

Creative Nonfiction • Jeanne Everhart

Yellow Marigolds bloom in a row of jigsaw shapes. They surround the water flowing from a fountain. I try to concentrate on color and shape to fill in all that is missing from this serene picture. For a few minutes I forget why I am here, and then remember it is not to put this puzzle together.

We wait, watching them come, one after another with pale skin, bald heads, and that slow halting walk of aging bodies. My fingers and eyes search for the puzzle piece with the right color green that matches the shape to make the landscape picture come together. This Cancer Center waiting room holds so many pieces. I cannot put them all together.

A silent prayer from my heart fills my thoughts as he is transfused with chemotherapy drugs. Oh God, let this medicine work to kill the cancer. This past year has been a roller coaster of emotion from diagnosis to treatment, with unending hope.

I put into place a piece of the water, reflecting purple and blue flowers, then pick up another dark blue piece but the shape doesn't quite fit. It is like the two months of intense chemotherapy confined in the hospital when we held on to hope for the miracle which almost worked, but treatment didn't quite fit. Hair gone, compromised immunity, muscles weakened and a little frail, he came home, with an incomplete picture of what the future holds. We are still searching for the pieces that will fit. How much can a body endure? We wonder what is going to happen next to a life that was so full and complete, but is now in pieces that do not go together as they should.

I stare at the blue sky puzzle pieces, sorting the white clouds and blue shades into piles. This is so confusing and sometimes becomes frustrating. Like the doctor that keeps trying new things, I keep trying new pieces to see if they work to finish this landscape. A TV monitor in my line of vision keeps flashing a smiling face and phone number for a Chaplin. I pick up another blue puzzle shape and tell a nurse nearby we are not going to give up. She says to keep fighting.

The last drop has been infused. There are still many pieces of the puzzle to put together. We will be back tomorrow.

The Day the Trees Came Down

Poetry • Stephanie Brown

First
I see trimmed boardwalk maples
and remind myself—*This was your
decision.*
It's hard to look at gaunt bodies
with gold caps that shade street
edges
where dog shit and deer scat
are found.

Next
I turn to our house on the hill,
tight grip on the wheel as my car
crawls up the driveway, spare sleeve
with no shadows from stray sumac,
tangled branches of birch
and red oak.

Then
sawdust graves become visible.
Shade garden is missing its muse,
its skeleton companion reduced
so now flavescent hostas peer
into the gap. *What have I
done?*

And
farther up, part of the squirrels'
playground and roof access is lost.
Four cavities remain where loyal
white oaks once cooled Chelsea
for thirteen summers, ninety-one
in dog years.

Now
where we used to place the kiddie
pool, under the shade of the black
walnut tree, another absence.
The tree had grown taller, lankier,
and leaned away from home,
as teenagers do.

Now
my knees buckle as I fall to the
ground,
claw at the ruined earth and plead
for winter to come, to weep
its white gauze over these fresh
sores.

Decisions, Decisions

Fiction • Sharon Harris

Shannon kept working, filing, keeping one eye out in the bank lobby through the big glass window. She never knew when he might come in. God, he turned her on. They had first kissed a couple of weeks ago, told each other how much they liked each other. They were shocked, stunned, horrified at what they felt. They were both married and agreed they did not want to hurt their spouses. But she had never been so excited, never felt so alive. Pierce was a silver-tongued devil—oh, the things he had whispered to her . . .

Shannon had always felt like she had a safe, perfect little life, all planned out. She had met one guy and was going to stay married to him forever. But oh, the pull she felt now—to stray, to touch, to feel and experience the things she had read about in all those damned romance novels.

She looked up again. There he was. Pierce. Even his name turned her on. She caught his eye and they both lit up, unable to keep from smiling broadly. Their looks held. He was well-known and well-liked in town, a successful businessman. Oh, that thick hair and trim beard. What a hunk. If you looked up "hunk" in the dictionary, his picture would be right there. All that dark hair and coffee-rich-with-cream skin—definitely her type. *Good grief.* How could everyone in the place not notice this spark, this intensity? If someone walked between them, they'd surely be badly burned. Moments passed as they eyed each other up and down. A teller waited on him.

"Shannon." She spun around. Her husband Terry stood in the doorway to the file room, his face pale.

"Oh, uh, hi." Shannon walked toward him. "What are you doing here?"

"We were supposed to meet for lunch." Terry swallowed, glanced at Pierce. "What's going on?"

"What? Nothing. What do you mean?"

"Shannon, I saw you looking at him." He stepped toward her. "What is going on?"

"What? No. Nothing." Shannon risked a glance at Pierce as she turned to get her purse. He finished with the teller, noticed Terry, put his head down, and strode for the door. *Chicken.*

Shannon heaved a sigh, kept her eyes firmly on Terry. "I've had a bad day, dear. I'm a basket case. Take me to lunch."

Lunch was silent. Her salad caught in her throat. Full of lustful thoughts lately, Shannon hadn't been able to eat and pounds had dropped off. Today though, her throat was completely closing up on her. *Oh my god. Poor Terry.* He'd never been a macho man. She knew he loved her beyond words even though he always had trouble telling her.

Terry wasn't eating much either. He kept smoothing the few strands of hair across the top of his head. Finally he shoved his plate aside, drank a few swallows from his glass of milk. He took a deep breath, his eyes on the table, and blurted out, "I know I'm not good enough for you, Shannon. But I've tried to be a good husband. What can I do to be better?"

Whoa. He is really worried. That was a long speech for him. Oh, the thoughts she'd had about Pierce, the things she'd wanted to do with him, the things he had said to her, the places in her that he had awakened. She felt like her eyes were floating. Images of the years of marriage with Terry, their kids, trips they'd taken—all of it swamped her. She pulled herself together with an effort. She'd call Pierce tomorrow.

"You can't do anything better, dear. You're the best."

Sapwood

Poetry • Hosanna Rasmussen

We are carving ourselves out of our births
products of myrrh and incense and a lick of oil
a drop of racism tucked behind our earlobes

a family tree of gnarled branches and sliced roots,
ginger and pine

the pulp of life kneaded under the sole of a foot
the curl of pipe smoke, from a Minnesota porch

tanned skin
dripping with water, dripping with hate
dripping with loyalty.

We are slowly and carefully carving our identities out of this soup,
and dragging our bread in it.

Flyover from 30,000 Feet

Poetry • Frances Ann Crowley

From the thrilling vantage point of my window seat,
the farmland below is plane geometry.
The pilot tells us this is where they grow the wheat for
Cheerios.

It is a grid constructed by the Homestead Act,
where roads and fences follow property lines,
producing orderly patterns on flat terrain.

I see an earth-toned patchwork of crop circles inside
squares surrounded by barbwire stitching;
a folk art landscape with plow lines like brush strokes
created by a tractor-crazy farmer-artist
using center pivot irrigation as his compass.

The Reader

Creative Nonfiction • Donna Uphus

I never saw my dad tinkering with the car or hunched over a wood-working bench. He read books, lots of paperback Western stories with tattered covers and dog-eared pages. He kept them in rumpled grocery bags behind the kitchen door within arm's length of his chair. His favorite author was Louis L'Amour and he loved the adventures of cowboys.

Some mornings I would get up very early, lean against the door jam, and watch him read. If he knew I was there, he gave no indication. The reader sat at the kitchen table with an open book. His left hand held the pages while his right would be up near his forehead, his boney fingers twirling a section of dark, thick hair. He wore a white V-neck T-shirt and the bronze skin on his thin arms and long neck looked seasoned, yet smooth like an animal hide turned into leather. One long leg would be crossed over the other at the knee, the dangling foot motionless. He'd have his black cowboy boots on as part of his everyday attire, even though he rarely went out in the cold of winter.

After what seemed like a long time, he'd switch the crossed leg, shifting his weight to the other hip. His left hand instinctively reached up to twirl the piece of hair and his right moved down to the book. He sat, long body pressed into the wooden chair, back curved over the table, and he bowed over the book. A dim, single naked light bulb hung over him, casting a shadow on the pages. His coffee cup sat near the open book, the liquid in it thick and black.

Smoking was always part of reading for the reader. The cigarette burned in the ashtray until he lowered the hand from his forehead and drew it to his lips, taking a long drag. His eyes squinted as the smoke swirled around his head. When the gray ashes fell onto the book, he'd turn it over, letting the ashes fall onto the table. He'd scoop them up and dump them into the overflowing ashtray that was always near his book. While the smoke tickled my nose and I didn't like the way it smelled, I couldn't pull myself away from where I stood and, if anything, I'd settle further into the spell I was under. He read, sitting still and quiet like a statue. After a little while he sensed my presence and said, "Hi, Sweetie," without looking back at me. My heart melted.

On Sunday nights in the summer months, my mother and I would pack his suitcase for the week's work out of town. He always chose two books to occupy his time spent in some cheap motel. He'd lay them on the bed next to his clothes and I'd hold them in my hands, leafing through the yellowed pages until my mother would tell me to put them on top of the clothes.

One winter an encyclopedia salesman came to our door and while my mother tried to discourage the man from making a sale, the reader turned into someone I didn't recognize. He ushered the man in, his face lighting up as if he'd won a tremendous prize. My dad pumped his hand vigorously and with little persuasion, he bought an entire set of books. I knew those books cost more money than our family had and it was rare for him to own much of anything, let alone a whole set of books. The reader was as excited as a child who just got a new bike for his birthday.

For the duration of the cold months that year and many to follow, I would see him reading those books, every one, cover to cover, silently sitting at the kitchen table. His curiosity of many subjects kept him reading and learning, but he didn't share what he knew. He carried the knowledge around locked in his head. While we rarely had conversations until late in his life, I knew my dad was very smart about many subjects and well-traveled without leaving the house.

When I grew up and married a farmer, books were what kept me from the loneliness and isolation that was so real as a farmer's wife and young mother. I read stories of other people's lives, putting myself in the place of the characters for solace. Did the stories bring my dad companionship and adventure like they did for me? Did he find himself in the characters he read about, like I did? Or did he simply love to read? I believe the answers are something we had in common.

As the years passed, anytime I stopped by my parents' house to visit, I'd find him sitting in his reading chair, a softer, more comfortable version now that he was older. His long legs were either crossed at the knees or the ankles in a familiar way. His beloved old boots rested next to the chair; his desire to wear them waned as he aged. The now wrinkled hand still reached up to his forehead, twirling the graying wisp of thinner hair between his fingers. His beloved Westerns were stacked in a neat pile on a small table beside his chair. His quiet words, "Hi, Sweetie," were music to my ears. He spent his days reading with one eye closed for lack of good vision, but he read nonetheless.

I share his love of books. While my dad owned few books, I find myself owning many. I have shelves of books and stacks of books and I read them all. I take after the reader, my dad. I read with unending passion, twirling a few strands of my hair with one hand, holding the book open with the other, just like he did. My dad is gone now, but the picture of him reading at the kitchen table remains in my mind's eye forever.

Du Fu Laments the Changing Landscape

Poetry • Justin Watkins

As a boy I had asthma
The only remedy was to walk
Amongst waves of grass
With my father, shooting pheasants

The dog's black lips were gentle
Holding shimmering feathers
We all understood our places
In the world

When I was fifteen the old dog died
And all the grass was plowed under
Our hunting lands grew quiet
And forbidden

I left to climb jade mountains
Taking words from high clouds
My bare feet grew worn with
Wandering

Now home again, gray and drinking
My house abandoned to the croppers
I bow my head at the window
Lamenting

My asthma has returned, the grass has not
Fingers of wine cling to green glass
And everywhere the tink tink
Of corn grains filling the coffers

My Youngest Uncle

Poetry Editor's Choice

• Kathryn Knudson

It might be grief, might be exhaustion
but I swear when I squint
my youngest uncle looks a bit
like Tom Selleck as Magnum P.I.
relocated to the Midwest and
gone slightly to seed.

In this narrow kitchen barely large
enough for two people to navigate
a Thanksgiving meal, my uncle used
to take on his nephews in games of Nerf
basketball, hoop clipped over the basement
door. He leapt and pushed and laughed
just as much as they did, disavowing—
hands held up as if innocent, head
shaking, eyes wide in mock
astonishment—trying to sell that
he had no part in creating the
new crack spidering the door.

He still laughs easily and deeply,
a sound that makes people turn
their heads, slight smile already playing
on their faces, his enjoyment infectious.

Tonight my youngest uncle walks
across the kitchen past a solid
basement door, Nerf hoop long since
lost, and sighs heavily
a trait we all seem to share—the ability
to say too much with just a breath.
He murmurs first with the hospice
volunteer then with the men
from the funeral home, while
the rest of us sit silently, hands
folded around cooling coffee cups.

First Call

Dad slid the sinker down the line, checked that the bobber stayed in place, and handed me my fishing pole. I dipped my hands into the bait bucket and pulled up a juicy fat leech. Just like my dad taught me to, I spit on him for good luck. I grabbed the pole and headed to the front of the boat where I liked to multitask as I fished. I would fish, soak up the sun, read, write, draw, sing, or just talk with Dad, in addition to baiting and setting the hook. Tonight, however, I had a much more specific goal on my fishing agenda.

Casting into shore, I landed my bobber right where I wanted it—halfway between the downed tree on the point and the moss-covered rock along the water's edge. "Nice work," Dad called out as he cast his own line behind the boat. My dad taught me everything I knew about fishing. My first excursions in the boat happened long before walking, talking, and bike riding. Now that I could hold my own fishing pole, pride filled me, knowing that I could cast like a pro with my open-faced spinning reel. I spent many hours on shore, casting just my line and a sinker, working on my accuracy, learning to work the bail, controlling the line, and testing the differences on the drag adjustments. My friends who fished used enclosed bait casting reels that rode on top of the pole with a thumb button and, as squeamish eight-year-old girls, they never hooked their own bait.

Dad sat in the back, messing with a knot in his line. Usually I felt lucky to get my line in the water before him, but this evening my mind focused on something else. I set my pole safely into the corner the bow seats made in the front of the boat, within easy reach—just in case my bobber sank and I had to abandon my practice and rush into fishing action. I had to figure it out now, I had to learn the trick of it before we returned to our city life. The front of the boat, the calm lake, provided perfect practice space.

With a sense of urgency, I cupped my empty hands together, just as I had seen my father do a million times out here on the lake, and I wiggled my fingers, adjusted my clasp, tightened the seal of my grip, brought the curve of my thumbs with their angled knuckles gently to my lips for a practice blow. I hoped to push the air from my breath into my clasped hands and produce a perfect lonely loon cry that would carry across the sunset-reflected waters and earn an answer from the loons across the lake. Reality brought only a rough spluttering sound far from the eerie cries my dad magically created.

Dad laughed, set down his pole, too, clasped his hands together, masterfully adjusted his grip, and solidly blew into his calloused and hardened thumb knuckles and presented the world his magic.

"You *are* getting better," he said. "Try again."

I did, again and again. I worked on creating a little loon magic of my own. I ignored my bobber, unconcerned that I hadn't even had a bite yet, and concentrated on hand placement, grip adjustments, and the force of my breath, right through my dad's first two fish of the night.

Tomorrow we would break down our camp and head back to town. The business of town activities would take precedent to quiet moments on the lake. Weeks might pass before hearing a loon call again. The family calendar and the garden in need of weeding nibbled away at my chances of success.

"Got another one!" I heard Dad announce, as he stood for his third attempt at fish.

"Go get him!" I encouraged.

The thrill of fish kept Dad from looking at me while I continued attempting to cast my magic. I coached myself through the setup, as my dad reached for the net. *Come on now, this is it, just-pursed lips, firm grip, solid inhale, you can do it.*

I brought my hands to my lips and Dad lifted the net from the water. He glanced at me, and I surprised us both with my first proud call of loon magic. A solitary loon across the water gifted me an answer just as the sun dropped down below the lake, and the best catch of the night landed in the boat.

Progression

Poetry Honorable Mention

• Marilyn Wolff

Mommy and Daddy said
You are so beautiful. Grow! Laugh! Love!
And she did.

Little brother said
Spend time with me, play ball, build forts.
And she did.

Teacher said
Remember these facts for there will be a test.
And she did.

Young husband said
You are so gorgeous and I love you so.
Wear these sexy clothes for me.
And she did.

Her children said
Be our biggest fan. Come to all of our games.
And she did.

Grandbabies giggled and laughed
Read us a book. Tell us a story.
And she did.

The disease said
Forget your entire life.
And she did.

Names of Prey

Poetry • Richard Fenton Sederstrom

We know we chased the fox away
by no more than our clumsy presence
on the track we call our drive.
The fat rodent we call a woodchuck
embraces the fragile safety of a pine.

But when I look back again at its
helpless face, its nibbling muzzle,
then I know in silence its true name
in the same way that I know its fear.
In that way too I know that:

if fear is a name we give it for a nonce,
then Fox, long disappeared into
the forest nethergrowth no longer needs
the name it has given itself to be what
the other knows it is. We embrace.

After Sauna

Poetry • Peggy Trojan

We came from sauna,
reddened, sweating.
Dave suggested
we sit on the deck
in the dark summer night,
in the drizzle,
stark naked
there in our woods.

Adjusting my bulk
to the unfamiliar webbing,
I laughed
at our impudence,
felt young,
strong and naughty.
Sat back,
and shamelessly
lifted my face
to the cooling rain.

Edna Lake circa 1994

Poetry • Justin Watkins

The pike were taken from dark
Water, by men in a rowboat
There were no other people
No lights or buildings or roads

The fish were made hot over fire
We leaned in, a three-man circle
Our heads centering on the food
Grimed eager faces in the heat

Fingers reached into the pan
Arms embraced plates on laps
The act is indeed an embrace
Of that which will become you

Lapping and wolfing sounds
Nods and low mumbling content
No words
Only fire, water and meat

Only the free and flowing savages
Dark in the dark night, understanding
Neither what we had achieved
Nor what was to come

Family Matters

Fiction • Nicole Borg

It was happening again. That low pain radiating up from the bottom of her belly just above her pubic bone, fingers of terrible pain reaching, doubling her over. She puts a hand on her stomach and the firm roundness is gone. Frantic, she tries to sit up, to call for her husband, but then she isn't in bed anymore. She's outside surrounded by trees. A forest. A rainforest. She doesn't know how she's gotten here. And the silence is so deep, so eerie, she can't breathe. There are birds and monkeys and eyes darting between the leaves but no sound. Everything is holding its breathing. Everything is waiting. And this terrifies her.

Mona opens her eyes. Coming out of this dream is like coming up from the bottom of a lake. It takes forever for her to surface, and when she does, the darkness clings to her. She tries to shake the sleep off. The phone is ringing and it sounds far away. Hank's side of the bed is empty. He is already at work. There is no bedroom clock but the sunlight pouring through the curtain tells her it's after 10:00. Mona tries to move faster. A hand strays almost absently to her belly. She's all but forgotten the details of the dream, but she has had this dream before, and it will stay with her all day. Mona gets to the phone just before the answering machine can pick up.

"Hello." Her voice is fuzzy with sleep.

"Is this Mona? Mona Reich?"

Mona doesn't recognize the woman's voice, but it isn't a telemarketer; there is too much hesitation, too little confidence. "Yes."

There is silence on the other end and Mona remembers the silence in her dream. Suddenly she feels dizzy and her heart is hammering in her chest. She puts a hand on the kitchen table to steady herself. "Hello?"

"Talon."

Talon. Talon. The baby. Her baby. No, not my baby. "Oh God. Has something happened?"

"Yes. No. Can you meet me somewhere?"

"Who is this?" Mona can barely speak. She is on the edge of hysterics. "Is Talon all right?"

The woman's voice becomes more sure. "Talon's okay. This is her grandma, Ruthie. We've met."

"Yes, I remember."

When Mary, Talon's birth mother came back to take the baby, Ruthie was with her, the woman from social services, and the police officer. Mona remembers that Ruthie wouldn't look at either her or Hank.

Ruthie wants to meet right away. Mona agrees. She can't imagine trying to sit down and have a cup of coffee or do the crossword puzzle, wondering what's going on with Talon. Better to meet now and be done with it. *I'll never be done with it.* Mona knows this is true. She doesn't have time to shower, only throws on a fresh outfit: a button up shirt and khakis. On her way to the car, she pulls out her cell phone and considers calling Hank. What would she say?

It's a park Ruthie has chosen for their meeting. Mona recognizes the irony in this. Childless after they took Talon back, Mona has no reason to go to parks. It only makes her bitter. All those mothers with their children, and she and Hank with no hope of having one on their own. She has never been to this particular park. It's in a sad-looking section of town, houses that need new roofs, sagging porches, cars parked where lawns should be. Two teens sit at an old picnic table and share what might be a cigarette or a joint. Mona parks the car but doesn't see anyone. Then she notices a woman in a straw hat with a scarf attached to it wearing large sunglasses and lurking by tall bushes. "No freaking way," Mona says aloud. The woman's disguise is straight out of a B movie.

The woman is Ruthie. She's like a stray cat, reluctant to get too close.

"Ruthie, it's Mona."

"Mona," the woman says and looks toward the picnic tables. The boys have wandered off and the two of them are alone. Not quite alone. Talon is in a stroller behind Ruthie, grape jelly on her face and a pacifier in her mouth. Mona's heart stops for just one moment.

Ruthie takes off her sunglasses. "I brought her. For you. I brought her here for you. I love my daughter." Her words are a jumble, so she starts again. "They're cooking again. I just know it."

"Cooking?" Mona asks, confused.

"Meth. Cooking meth. That good-for-nothing boyfriend and her. He's out of jail. It's only a matter of time before they get arrested or blow the place up or worse. And I can't—I brought some clothes but that's it. I can't keep her. Mary'd just come back for her." Ruthie stops and looks hard at Mona. "You want her still, right?"

"I—"

"You know how it'll turn out for Talon. Mary made a mistake taking that little girl back. You and your husband were a blessing for Talon. Mary loves her, but it doesn't stop her from being a bad mom. I brought Talon's teddy bear, Bearly, and her blankie, the one I made. But that's it. Mary doesn't know I took her." Ruthie's glances are filled with one part terror and two parts determination. She pushes the stroller at Mona. "You'll take her?"

The park is silent. Mona is caught in this silence, watching herself and watching the woman Ruthie who is smuggling her granddaughter to

Mona. Mona's heart is a bomb in her chest. But there is only one thing for her to say. Hank would know what it was. "Yes."

There is no car seat. Mona can hardly get past this. She's transporting a baby without a car seat. "A stolen baby," she whispers, as she settles the little girl into a nest of blankets on the passenger floor and almost laughs hysterically. If she starts, she won't be able to stop. Mona tosses the umbrella stroller into the trunk. When she starts the car, Talon only looks up at her with those wide hazel eyes. Ruthie is gone, disappeared after handing Talon over.

Mona is sure she is too nervous to drive, but the driving calms her. Talon settles into her nest of blankets and is asleep before Mona gets on the freeway.

They will have to go somewhere. She and Hank and Talon. They can't stay here. Someone will surely come looking for Talon, won't they? But it doesn't matter. They will do whatever they need to. Mona has her family back. And there is nothing she ever wanted more.

No Goodbye

Poetry • Vincent D O'Connor

Twisted metal and
shattered bones

a cruel
announcement.

How had they the heart
to leave such heaviness
at my door?

How to lift it?

Where to lay it down?

I call again
but
your voice still says
you are not there.

The Promised Land

Poetry • Audrey Kletscher Helbling

My father hefts a seed corn bag from the earth,
pours a stream of pink-tipped kernels into the planter,
fires up the John Deere, settles onto the seat,
then putters toward the field black as coal.
Good rich farm land, they say. None better.

I've listened to crops grow in Redwood County
on a sweltering Minnesota summer afternoon,
when my father surveyed row upon row
and wiped away a ring of grimy sweat trapped
beneath the winged ear of his DEKALB cap.

In the slight stir of a July morning,
I've heard sharp-tongued corn leaves whisper
as our detasseling crew swept across the acres,
our hands stretched to grip and yank tassels,
dew streaming from fingertips to armpits.

Memories root me to this land of my youth,
to three generations of farmers who clasped hands
in prayer for rain, then felt the unwelcome cool
of a storm bearing hail, destroying hope
with amens still clinging to sun-parched lips.

Yet they clung, like I do, to this promised land,
souls freed by untethered wind and open spaces
broken only by the occasional grain elevator—
cathedrals of the prairie—held in high reverence
by those who strive to attain the harvest.

Step Stool

Poetry • Cheryl Weibye Wilke

I want a step stool for my birthday. That's all.
Solid oak. One step up to where I want
to go. No confusion about what purpose

it serves. A no-nonsense step stool. It can be
old, but it must be stable. No wobble. Painted
or stained. One I can easily carry from the kitchen cupboards,

to bedroom closet and office bookshelves. Light,
but well-made. Not temperamental. One that remembers
my burgeoning weight. Shrinking

height. Achy back. Tremble. And what is in store
where: the Christmas china, mixing bowls, favorite sweatshirts, scarves, purses and poems. One

that can help me make the final stretch.

Untamable Things

Poetry • Tarah L Wolff

The last thing you will
see of me
will be my pony tail swaying
behind my head
as I kick off my shoes
and shed this
cotton and nylon
skin as I finally
run

And the only thing you will ever
see of me again
will be my eye shine
from the ditch
when your
headlights perchance
to reflect back at you from
me

You will turn your wheel very hard
and gasp
*Look! I've never seen one in the wild
before!*
You will capture me for
just
long enough
for you to say
It's a woman!
before I am gone
and you will want me
and you will hunt
me

Carving the Burl

Poetry • Ruth Schmidt-Baeumler

Pints fit in the glove compartment,
inner pocket of a tight-fitting pea coat,
outer left-hand pocket of the gray-green hunting jacket,
under the driver's car seat,
in the lunch pail,
slit in the boat seat,
tackle box,
scratched blue-gray accordion tool box below the first level.

Quarts fit between two studs
in the unfinished garage, outdoor biffy,
and dirt-floor storage area,
behind the furnace, the dryer, the bed post,
in rubber boots needed only when it rains,
tucked between sweatshirts or underwear.
One quart always visible on the kitchen
counter, Sunny Brook welcoming him home.

When they give him the choice of losing
his job or going to detox, he chooses
the jitter ward to sweat toxins out of his body,
hallucinations out of his mind.

After two weeks of determination he is
already released, brings home a
beautiful wooden salad bowl carved
in therapy sessions out of birch burl.

When she sees him again the rules
of communication have changed.
Relevant comments replace years
of non-interest.

She waits, not trusting this truce,
waits for things to return to normal,
to slip back
into the familiar childhood formula.

Touching Wild
Creative Nonfiction • Michael Forbes

The morning sky is full of hot July blue. Beyond the edge of our yard coppery grasses shine in a field gone wild with sunlight and neglect, gone wild with the freedom to be a field and nothing else. On this morning after the Fourth, the neighborhood is quiet. No mowers, no leftover firecrackers, no dogs chopping the stillness into bite-size chunks. Only a few vesper sparrows buzz from the shadows under the pines.

Last night Karen and I fished the river, letting the heat of the day slip away as we waded in the slow current, trying to lure a trout into our world. Fishing for trout is not the only reason we visit this river. Mostly Karen and I go just to look at some living thing, flowing, inviting and yet, out of reach.

At the river we parted, each seeking a promising stretch of water that might deliver what we wanted. For Karen the river often means otters as well as trout. Symbols of fluid grace and strength, either one is reason enough to return. One mocks you out loud. The other flips you off, refusing your dry fly with the flick of a spotted tail. Karen is not above asking the river for an otter. Last night she came close, finding a perfect paw print in the soft mud at the water's edge. For me the river was not about trout or otters; it was about my need to be in the wild.

I walked far upstream before entering the river. The evening was still too bright for the trout and too hot for me so I stood in the water, waiting. While my fly drifted in lazy S-curves below me, a summer-red doe parted the green curtain of grass. Stepping into the river, each movement precise and sure, she embodied the perfect choreography of need. Pausing when the mirror of water rose to her belly, she dipped her neck just enough and drank. Later Karen told me she had also seen a deer. Hers was a buck, with velvet-covered antlers swelling into knobby forks. Moving his head side to side, the buck stared down the length of his nose at the yellow-shirted intruder in his river. From three rod lengths away, he regarded my wife. Karen's intent was pure. No deer yet has reason to fear my wife armed with a fly rod.

When the trees grew tall enough to hide the sun and a slight chill shimmered through the river bottom, I hooked a trout. After waiting through the heat of the day in deep shade, this rainbow, green flank flashing, rose to take my fly. The advantage was all his. He shook free but not before I felt his weight pulsing in the river. Casting again, I hooked and lost another trout: maybe the same one. It didn't matter. I caught. I lost. I laughed.

Keeping pace with the advancing twilight, I moved slowly downstream. Where a cornice of willows and alders hung over the river, I hooked another trout. Pulling in a way known only to his kind, he yanked my old bamboo rod into a throbbing arc. I felt every shake of the head, every roll and twist of his body run up the line connecting us to one another. He dug hard for the bottom of the river and safety, but I knew he was mine. A strong fish. I had to let the force of the current tire him out before he would allow himself to be moved against his will.

When at last this perfect manifestation of spirit lay shining silver in the last light of day, I cradled him in my wet hands. I could've lost this trout and that would've been fine. When he was ready I removed the hook, opened my fingers and the river took him in. Sometimes we just need to touch the wild we seek and hold it in our hands a moment before letting it slide back into the dark waters.

Vigil

Poetry • William Upjohn

Woolsey Pond

The pond's calm water mirrors the thin-rimmed moon,
a still-life framed by our window, opened wide
to invite Spring's incense and sound-laced air
inside. To drift through our room,

scattering lilac and other fragrances,
sipped and lifted, stashed in a satchel
of nature's greenings—greetings
to stir our over-wintered senses.

Side-by-side in bed, we are settled. Below
your deep breaths, I imagine you submerged
in resplendent gardens, enveloped in scents.
But I lie wide awake, breathing slow, listening:

baritone tree frogs and tenor peepers calling out
different versions of the same ancient song.
The toads, an ordered chorus, chant
in rising trill

and pause.
Green frogs gasping
low and floppy,
hopeful solos.

Faint, succinct: something rustling
the cattails. A sudden splash in the pond.
I rise from bed, lean out the window,
try to catch the movement by moonlight.

Clouds float in, slowly crossing the pond.
The half-ring of moon wanes,
then fades, from the water's rim.
Light rain starts to fall

on the leaves.
Fingers of wind
brush the treetops,
stir the still air.

A bird's cry, shrill,
in the distance.
Then, close, suspended—
silence.

If I should turn
away, who will remain
as witness? This night, so wide.
How could I sleep?

Two is Company

Poetry • Sreekanth Bhaskaran

Body wizened and eyes sunken—this is really not you but just your ghost.
You joke that it is a diet fad and laugh; the pills on the windowsill laugh too.
There is a halo around your still handsome face, a calm bearing of knowing
what is to come, what has passed and making peace with every part of it.

"Will you stay for one more meal?" you plead. There is a juicy steak in the
        fridge
bought on food stamps; you saved it for me. "We will just lounge on the
        couch,
say nothing if you do not want to, stare at the ceiling or flip through
        magazines.
No regrets," you say. "It was a life well-lived," but "Will you stay for just one
        more meal?"

You were once the life of the party, laughing loudly, throwing your head back;
you stood tall and dashing, confident know-it-all, consummate do-it-all.
Every boy and girl wanted to be your friend, to dance with you, listen to you
        sing.
They tried to brush by you while you filled your drink just to get a whiff of you.

Today in this small white apartment, your framed cheerful photos mock from
        the wall,
the sun streams in through dirty windows onto wilting plants, old books strewn
        around.
A bicycle stands in the corner sulking, gathering dust. I gather my coat, get to
        the door.
You look up from the couch and ask one more time, "Will you stay for just one
        more meal?"

Every Drop of Water is the Ocean

Poetry • Peter William Stein

Stellar phytoplankton paint
a milky sea effect
across a black canvas

The light drips,
blue cools, red excites,
green calms, yellow hungers,
greys are patient,
they only differ
in wavelength

I bathe in these hues
constantly washing ashore,
blend my own wet sensations
into the fabric.
I would look inward
if there were such a thing

I peer out toward
the lost and lonely islands,
peaks of a vast landscape
beneath a fluid surface,
their forms defined by
where the waves break

The sky takes in
a deep breath of ocean,
clouds the earth, consumes
the fire rising on the horizon,
erases the difference
between water and air

I am submersed in this ocean
that has no surface
I cannot swim but have learned
to take on water

Deer Tracks

Creative Nonfiction • Deb Schlueter

One of those rare, beautiful January days had finally arrived. The temperature warmed to *almost* not freezing, the sun glinted off newly fallen snow, and the wind had died. After endless days of indoor recess, arctic wind chills, and mid-year testing stress, I took the opportunity to bundle my kids—all twenty-five of them—in their winter gear and take them for a walk in the woods behind the school.

We got to be the first to make footprints in the thick, white blanket lying on the football field. Kids raced from side to side, making crazy zigzag patterns in the snow. Now and then one would drop down to make a snow angel. Still too cold for snowballs, some students contented themselves with lobbing armloads of powder at each other.

As we neared the tree line, the kids grew quiet. Our goal was to locate winter wildlife—to find the creatures brave enough to withstand a harsh Minnesota winter. We knew noise would scare them off; however, sneaking through the woods with two-dozen kids was not easy. Snow pants and thick jackets swished in the quiet. The snow crunched and squeaked against boots. Kids giggled and whispered. Our breath fogged in the air around us.

"Oh look, oh look," one of them whisper-yelled, pointing with a mitten. He'd found our first sign of life—a small chickadee hopping from branch to branch on a red oak. Dead leaves clung to the branches and rustled as the bird moved. A dozen pairs of binoculars trained on the bird before someone correctly identified it.

Soon we were into the thick trees and the world came to life around us. Birds fluttered, perhaps looking for remnants of the students' pinecone bird feeders. Squirrels raced around the pine trees, chattered at us, and swished their tails. When someone pointed out winding sets of tracks in the new snow, we kept watch for anything that might have made them.

One set of tracks in particular had the kids' attention. Deer tracks led across the clearing where our school had set up some picnic tables and an outdoor stage. Several students were craning their necks to see past the trees. A few industrious girls broke away from the group and silently traced the tracks towards the bushes to see where they went.

Flying snow erupted from the bushes just feet in front of them. The girls stumbled backward, startled screams echoing through the trees as a white-tailed deer exploded from the bushes. The rest of us frozen in surprise, the deer was little more than a flash of brown and white as it bounded past us —almost near enough to touch—before it vanished into the trees.

The encounter was over in a second. The shocked silence that had descended on our group lasted a few seconds longer. Then the kids started to giggle.

The girl who'd been closest to the deer pushed herself up and raced to my side, eyes wide, hurriedly explaining what had just happened to her—like I hadn't been ten feet away, watching. "Did you see that?" she told her classmates with a huge grin. "I almost stepped on a *deer!*"

"Look!" one of the boys added, edging to the bushes where the deer had lain and found the place it had been curled up. "You can see some of the fur it left behind."

Another boy glared at the girls who had startled the deer, looking truly annoyed. "You scared its fur off! Now it's gonna freeze."

We examined the deer's resting spot—a few students eying the remaining bushes warily—before continuing our trek down to the pond, around the shore, and then back up to the school. The students were quiet, no doubt hoping to find some other neat creatures hiding in the snow. But a few squirrels, birds, and one lonely rabbit were all we found.

When the students were back in class and chronicling their walk, many drying out wet socks and warming cold fingers, the deer featured in almost every story. Pictures were drawn and a name was decided upon. Only one student had found something more interesting than the deer: he'd spent the entire walk counting pinecones.

Stopping By the Side of the Road

Poetry • Kari E Hagstrom

Got to pull over. Now.
Or those runaway
thoughts will disappear,
never to be heard from
again. Harness them,
capture them between a sharp
point and this sheet of paper.
Got to write.
Now.

Park on an approach.
Put this old rusted red
Chevy truck in park,
with its dog-chewed seats
and sprung-door
that lets in the wind.
Leave the engine running:
it's still winter.

Find a piece of paper.
Something.
Anything.
A bank envelope,
anything that will hold ink.
Take the envelope apart
for more room, more
blank space to fill.

As urgent as sex,
as pressing as birth,
as timely as death.
Do it now.
Reach
before it flies
out the door.
Write it now.
Now.
Before it's gone.

Bittersweet Beans

Poetry • Charmaine Pappas Donovan

Remembering Jane Galloway (1956-2013)

In the kitchen working on a pot of first-ever
baked beans made from scratch,
thick-cut bacon wrinkling in the pan
gives off such a warm smoky smell
my husband must snatch a slice
before he leaves the house to golf.

Here, in the middle of cutting onions,
not needing their vapor to rise to my eyes
and make me cry, I think of Jane at home
only a few miles up the road
on hospice, I've been told,
because her cancer has spread.

I think of her early adoption,
how she had only a spotty health history,
ways we shared jobs and offices together.
Conversations took us on circuitous paths
as we pondered life's meaning,
offering one another olive branches of hope.

I stand at the cutting board,
turn away from the mound of chopped onions
I need to make baked beans for tomorrow.
I ponder my friend's shortening life,
grateful for my good health, good fortune,
that crisp smell of bacon tingling the air.

Summer's Skirmish

Poetry • Linda M Johnson

John Deere is freshly oiled and gassed up.
The old Model LT 155 has done this drill
thousands of times but runs just fine
not ready to retire from service just yet.
Its lone troop, armored with bug dope
safety glasses and earplugs,
adjusts his ball cap, starts the engine
and thus begins another battle
in summer's war.

The fescue and bluegrass mix
covering the yard is neutral territory;
a slight trim off the top improves
the uniform look of the lawn.
But the enemy is not shy—
offensive yellow-headed helmets
profusely populate the landscape.
As the mower methodically navigates the lawn
each pass slightly overlaps the last.
Nothing left to chance; beheading begins.
As the foe is ruthlessly sliced in two
a cunning few hear the drone
of the old John Deere and they duck,
avoid rotating blades by a mere petal-breath.
Once danger has passed they rise up
salute the sun, toss their seed,
vow never to be defeated.

Anthem

Poetry • Jeanne Emrich

It's November.
The cold wants into the house.
Outside, the aspens are singing
their anthem of leaves, of what we give
and do not give to this world.
I count my words now—
those I have lost or doubted or
abandoned like unwanted children.
How few have I trusted to carry
my bare heart in their arms
or believed in enough to let fall
into my life and scatter,
making their own meanings.
All day I have waited for the snow,
for the flurries that fall thousands
of feet but can't be seen until
just before they land—
beautiful, wayward, unpredictable—
like words I don't know until I speak them,
words I promise myself to trust.

Cleaning After a Funeral

Poetry • Susan Niemela Vollmer

I spend this day of the snowstorm
Running a steamer back and forth
Across my living room carpet

There is comfort in this mindless routine
A repetition that mimics
The steadily falling snow

Press the button and water flows
The machine smoothly
Pulls the used water back up

Clearing the storm's results
Will be a more difficult task
The remnants heavy and clinging

Soon toddlers will crisscross this floor
Much as my mother crossed it over the years
Generations of unsteady foot traffic

The machine draws up the detritus
As gray as my mother's old bones and ashes
Soon to be scattered and settled like snow

Hospice

Your daughter was married in that
chalk-white church
on 4th street; the scaly black roof, the greening.
And that picture of me in a
dark suit and white shirt
standing by the curb with
buck teeth and bangs.
I was eight then but now fifty and eight.
Some Sundays Dad had me
place hymn numbers in the oaken racks.
I wore the red and white
acolyte
robes to light
candles at pew ends and on the carven alter.
And you kneeling at the rail as the priest
dipped the host into a silver chalice shining
with red, red wine and placed it on
your baby bird tongue.
And one day the bishop thumbed
a cross of oil on my kneeling forehead.
All this was so
long ago
and I wonder if it now floats
in your bed-
ridden
head.

Umbrellas

Poetry • Mary Willette Hughes

This rainy spring day near the D. C. Senate building a noontime bouquet of opened umbrellas flourish their bold red, yellow, blue and green nylon fabric, tautly stretched across curved metal ribs. Umbrellas blossom on stalk handles, sway in May wind and are held by working women whose faces are hidden, who stop at the corner to chat, who wait for traffic to halt. The semaphore greens; the bouquet walks on trim stem-legs, crosses the street, separates into single blooms, and hurries off in different directions to flower the foyers of drab office rooms. When raindrops dry, each opened umbrella will be folded into itself and placed in a waiting, upright reliquary, earth-colored and elegant, enduring in carved design.

Some Days Poems are Everywhere

And they practically announce themselves,
Rocketing around like kids piling out of the schoolhouse, or
Zooming toward you like a peleton of bikers carving a corner
At some ungodly perilous angle,
Or the hoarse honking of geese winging across the marsh,
Or a passel of ants swirling and scurrying on the sidewalk,
Or the air wafting across the grass, or the leaves—
Oh, man, the leaves: Summer green riot of chlorophyll
And energy synthesizing, doing all the work for you, or
Fall leaves trembling to be adored before they
Let go. And there's rain, stringing down and bounding off the
Deck furniture, and clouds lowering, snow murmuring,
Night dropping, dawn rising, crowds weeping with joy
On election night. All poems, just everywhere, so
You unlock the door and invite them in.

Fireweed

Trees. Trees, trees, and more trees. I think they might be some kind of spruce, but what would I know?

I bet you know what they are. You know everything, Jack. You know why my leg itches. You know what those stupid purple flowers are. You know which mountain that is and why I'm standing next to a lake that is not on my map.

This is all your fault. Stop looking like that—this was *completely* your idea. A guy's weekend camping, away from the wives, just like when we were kids. Fishing in Alaska, wouldn't that be fun?

And yeah, I thought it would be. I've always wanted to be like you, you know. Older cousin, the one everyone likes, the guy who can fix a car with some duct tape and chewing gum and look good while doing it. But who was I kidding?

Look at me, Jack. Do you know what I paid for these clothes? Camping equipment I'll never use again? I don't even know what half of this stuff is—just that you said I'd need it. This thing? This metal, box . . . thing? What could this even be?

Don't think I was fooled. I knew you were using the little rich cousin to buy you a bunch of new toys. I just let you.

What kind of lousy person am I? Allowing you to run over me, simply because you're popular and good looking and . . . You've done it all my life, so why am I so surprised?

But what does it matter, anyways? Because here we are. At a random lake in Alaska. Camping. Absolutely *wonderful*.

The bugs stink, by the way. If you so much as mention bears, I will do my best to feed you to the fish regardless of what your wife would want. Apparently the salmon are running.

I didn't even know "salmon" was a real type of fish until now. I mean, I *knew* it was a fish, but I figured it was along the lines of fish sticks and fish sandwiches. I didn't realize you could *catch* a salmon. I kind of thought you were joking, until we got here and you handed me that fishing rod.

It's your fault. You wanted this, not me. I don't like it out here.

Just to be clear, I stopped liking the outdoors when I figured out you could read about the outside while safe at home with a cup of hot chocolate. Or maybe it was the night at summer camp when you stuck all those leeches to me while I slept.

Maybe I should have taken it as a sign: I'm the cosmic butt of your stupid jokes. How many leeches can I stick to him before he wakes up? How many times will he let me take him paintballing before he realizes I'm setting him up? How many times . . .

Do you know, Jack? I knew it the first time. I knew it *before* the first time, but I let you run over me anyways. Over and over and over. Because you're my cousin. Because I'm a weak-minded imitation. Because everybody likes you and if I stayed around long enough, they'd like me too.

I was going to tell you, when we got here, that I knew about the affair. I had it all planned out in my head—what I was going to say, what I was going to do . . . But you know how big of an idiot I am? I was going to let you keep sleeping with my wife. I was going to let you because . . . I don't even know why.

You know what? You can just quit. I don't care if she leaves me. I don't care if that costs me my job since my boss likes you more than me. You know why?

Because you dragged me on this fishing trip. Because you had to have a heart attack and leave me here, alone. Yeah, you Jack. Staring dead at the mountains. Lying there, surrounded by those stupid purple weeds like some sort of god.

What a joke. You're no god. You're just a dead guy I let ruin my life. When the rescue people track my cell phone signal and drag your body out of here, I'm not going to your funeral. I'll be the only person in a twenty-mile radius not there . . . but I won't be there. This, here in the middle of nowhere, is your eulogy from me. A shadow, speaking in the wind, where nobody but the bugs can hear. It's probably more than you deserve.

You know what else? I found the matches you said you weren't going to bring, because "real guys" know how to start fires without matches. How many times have you secretly lit the campfires with matches, telling us you didn't? How many times . . .

What a joke, Jack. You know I found the matches *after* I got the fire going. You know what that makes me?

And you know what that makes you?

Traveling Amtrak by Night

Poetry • Nicole Borg

Dad, I thought I saw you
on the 7 Empire Builder
leaving from Red Wing—
your body grown too thin,
walking down the aisle
off balance, a step away
from disaster. You spoke too
loudly into your cell phone,
giving too many details—
almost homeless, between
jobs, seven dollars to your name.
It didn't surprise me that
your luggage was four
black garbage bags knotted
at the top which you gathered
while we waited for the train
to debark two hours late
at Fargo Station. You smelled
faintly of cologne, and while
I stood with the baby in
my arms and my duffel bag
and his diaper bag at my
feet, you smiled and asked
how old he was and said he
sure was cute. Your laugh,
when it came, was easy,
and that was the only way
I could be sure that the man
on the train wasn't you.

Last Hunt with My Father

Poetry • Sandra Evans

The sun setting
every hair in white
relief—we are
surrounded by shadows
but the road is made of
strands of light.

He walks with the gun
broken over his arm
like an ermine stole
nothing like Henry the VIII.
We have a rhythm, grass crushing
anything outside register
my eyes follow the trajectory
of my dad's gaze and extend it
to the rotten trunk
where the male has just
mounted, ready to drum
the thrum just starting
a heartbeat gone viral
until it stirs our guts like
heavy bass.

Even though
it will mean we're skunked
my dad will not fire the rooster
as he calls out for love
from the tender heart
of Koochiching.

Shelter Me

Poetry • Laura L Hansen

Every couple of days of this endless winter
the wind sculpts new patterns on the snow
and ice-bound river. Last week's pockmarks
are smoothed over and reformed into elegant scrolls
and again this morning after a screaming north wind
the river has a new skin, only a few
of her old wrinkles showing.

The long arc of a snowbank cleaves
the backyard in two, overwhelms the white
lawn chair left out on the patio last fall.
Trees have deep wells around their stiff-legged
trunks, wells so round and perfect
that I long to shelter there, curled up
as tight as a napping cat.

The Lady's Slippers

Poetry • Steven R Vogel

The lady's slippers must be left outside;
They must be worn only on moss.
They must step only in places
No one has stepped before,
Where no pink, or green,
Or white silk thread
Has tangled life,
Or left a mark.

Lovely steps
Begin and end
Outside the doors,
Outside the realm of weavers
Who run straightened, shortened lines.

Putting the Party to Bed

Poetry • Ryan W Keller

The bees lay bumbled by their mead.
The bear has tucked himself in early too,
after stealing too much of a buzz from the bees.
Deer run tipsy through the woods,
full of grain and barley.
The butterflies are all fluttered out
from the sweet taste of dandelion wine.
Squirrels and field mice still chirp and chatter
over who gets to finish the last corn whiskey.

A white flurry hangover is on the horizon,
and the party lies depleted.
The good mother comes to tuck us in.
We will awake to a white noise headache,
savoring our regrets from the summer beers.
But I am not quite ready for bed yet.
I am staying awake with our mother.
I raise my vodka soda in salute,
drawing flavor from a cigar.
Let our mother never say
I left her to party alone.

Wheel Barrow

Poetry • Rebecca Ramsden

Most of the time, it camps on two legs
waiting in the shed until duty calls
when my father lifts solid oak arms
pushing the load to fill wet depressions

in the driveway. Once the haul is dumped
I climb inside, sit cross-legged, hands grip
to slanted sides, bracing for a wild ride.
Anticipation rises with all balance on one

wheel, flexible functionality pivots
sway left, lean right, I squeal with delight.
Over the course of varied cargo, cinder
block etchings, gravel scratches and
shovels full have sanded the metal bare.

Back at the shed we fluff brushes, mix
paint. My Van Gogh strokes sweep wide
lacquer black gloss—later thin brush red
opens petals abloom on outer walls.

In 91 years, how many loads has he carried—
outworn the rusty ride, layers beyond shadows.
Look around at the whole family—each one
carried safely home to honor his day.

Flash of Yellow

Poetry • James Bettendorf

It was a small bird
its long confident beak
a yellow compass pointing home.
Was it a Common Yellowthroat,
a Goldfinch maybe

or a Yellow-rumped Warbler?
How could I convince it
I meant no harm, my only desire
a closer look to know for certain
what kind of bird it is.

It flitted away as I approached,
just like the girls in yellow dresses
at my junior high school dance
when I set foot on
their side of the gymnasium.

The Treadmill

Poetry • Kim A Larson

Like a displaced conveyer belt from
some archaic assembly line, he stands,
incomplete, dreaded beast. Lacking enjoyment
and stirring up remorse, a monstrosity
of guilt. A reminder of resolutions,
failed and futile. Like a hard-to-swallow
pill, an act of prevention. Monotonous
as an endless road.

We met out of need—I to use, and he
to be used. We were fast, furious, and frequent.
But repetition breeds boredom, and I tired
of our routine rendezvous leading
nowhere. Spring sprang. I roamed.
The world outside, inviting. The grass
quivered, the sky floated, the air
exhaled, and the sun exploded. No more
black tread, odors of suppers past, white
ceiling overhead, and forced-air gas.
I was going places. He, stationary,
collecting discarded clothing at home.

The grass browned, the sky melted, the air
bit, the sun retreated. My path led back to
my less-traveled friend, where need supersedes
desire. I welcomed familiarity like a warm
bath on a cold winter night, and savored
predictability as if it were the last sip
of hot chocolate. He posed no questions, passed
no judgments, portrayed no disappointment.
He was content. For when used,
he was complete.

Eggs and Bread

Fiction • Audrey Kletscher Helbling

He shuffles into line, hands clenched upon cart handle, milky eyes cast down.

Inside the wire basket, he's placed a half-gallon of two percent milk, a loaf of white bread, a cylinder of old-fashioned oats, a dozen eggs and a carton of vanilla ice cream. The basics. Nothing more, nothing less.

He glances at his worn Red Wing work shoes, at the yellowed tile floor, then raises and skims his eyes across magazines. Around him voices drone. He remains oblivious, caught in his thoughts, until a toddler's cry pierces the monotony of sound.

His head pivots. An unruly gray curl brushes his forehead, a reminder that he needs a trim.

A boy, perhaps two, with flaming red hair and green snot smeared across his left cheek, leans toward Albert from the seat of his mother's shopping cart. He shrieks with arms flailing, for Albert, anyone, to rescue him.

Albert focuses on the toddler, feels the tension ease from his shoulders, his hands reflexively releasing from the cart. He wants to reach out, to touch the softness of the child's pudgy hands, to feel the whisper of a memory. Their first-born. Their son.

But he stops, catches himself, turns his head back toward the check-out line, to the disinterested teen scanning bar codes, the bagger shoving groceries inside plastic bags for a thirty-something woman chattering on her cell phone.

He begins setting his purchases onto the counter—the milk first, then the ice cream and oatmeal followed by the eggs and bread. Just like she instructed him.

"Paper or plastic?" he deciphers through the fog of emotions that dim his senses.

"Paper," he rasps, clears his throat and repeats. "Paper."

He pulls a tattered checkbook from the back pocket of his bib overalls, scrawls his name across the bottom of a State Bank check, tears the slip out and hands it to the checker. She hesitates, uncertain, understands, then inks in "The Corner Grocery Store" and "$11.08."

"Have a good day." She passes the receipt to Albert, fails to meet his eyes before moving on to the next customer.

He reaches for the paper bag, clasps it to his chest, remembers Elsie's hugs. The last one. The moment he understands. Shallow breathing. Quickened sense of urgency. The instructions about eggs and bread and laundry and Nona next door paying his bills. The everyday details, ever so precise, presented over a period of months.

As he lumbers to his Chevy, tears threaten. Albert's throat tightens. He unlatches the rear driver's side door, settles the bag of groceries onto the seat, closes the door.

Albert pauses. He sucks in air, opens the driver's door, eases behind the wheel. He knows he's done right by Elsie. The eggs and the bread. Always last.

Haiku

Poetry • Kristin F Johnson

Loss weighs down our limbs
heavy branches under snow
waiting for spring thaw.

Tissues

And I am mute
looking at her—a hundred
years between us almost
and it feels like that many generations
at least
with utterly no idea how to bridge them
her skin has become as thin as the
tissues she tucks into
her sleeve

I leave the music playing on
opposite ends of the house so
I will not have to walk into silent
and I wish I knew if
that would have been her choice at my age if
she feared silence too or if broken hearts
were actually silly back then
as I suspect
as everyone makes out

And I am mute as she is blind
(there are no more questions to impose upon her)

She's holding my hand now
and I want to ask her
all these things
if she smoked to run like I do
and drank to run sometimes too
(like I do) from a broken heart
or if this is all silly
as I suspect
as everyone makes out
or maybe as she
is now is more like as
she was then
(like me)
as thin and fragile
as the tissues she tucks into
her sleeve

Proof

Poetry • Christy Gove-Berg

On the night
That I held you on the sidewalk
Fat cheek pressed to mine
Eyelashes brushing my face
And together
We looked skyward
To the moon
Cradled crescent
By the dark deep sky
Sung lullabies by
Jupiter and Venus
Their two bright eyes watching over
The smallness of us
As we existed there
Silent
Together

And in that moment
I believed
Utterly.

For how else are fat cheeks,
And long baby eyelashes,
Warm breath like tinsel in cold air,
And a perfect trio shining high in the night sky
Possible?

A Thousand Miles

Creative Nonfiction • Shasha C Porter

Sifting, fingers searching for the feel of it, from the recesses of the glove compartment of the car—the small yellow calculator. Thinking. Trying not to think. *Interesting, that we continue to refer to the glove compartment as "the glove compartment."*

Shifting the visor to block the sun's glare. Sitting in the driveway, ignition off. Multiplying days, miles. *Could've used the cell phone to calculate;* yet, would take longer to figure out how to save time using the "cell" than to enter numbers with these more concrete clicks.

What is the distance from lost to found? The number of miles . . .

Miles of driving of a far different sort than to skating lessons, to snow boarding, or to the dentist. Innocent trips, those. Innocuous. While driving to the Addiction Treatment Program for Youth was about navigating earliest morning traffic in the heated haze of late summer, always against the clock, trying not to miss the exit. Again.

Slowing in the speed zones, eyeing the turn to the left missed more than once. A turn near-to invisible from the road, appearing only when nearly blown past it, if not intently seeing. Then, the U-Turn.

Admitting

Coming to

Winding down the long, unevenly surfaced, wooded road, spurious rough spots making the tires bump. Learning to anticipate the rough spots. Slowing down.

Making a decision

The repeat drive to pick her up from her day of *wanting to want* recovery; that's what she said.

The afternoon's rush hour; driver's fingertips tapping steering wheels, impatient with the metered entrances. Waiting. *Trust the light.* It turns for each.

Repeat. The next morning. The next. Through weeks and worries and non-comprehending denial disorientation. *I am trying to avoid the words abject fear.*

Leaving her for an hour's meeting on a Friday evening, walking up the steps from the basement of the community building overhearing the words spoken aloud: "My name is—and I'm an addict." I stop on the top step, stilled. The words hit my heart like an arrow.

I admitted—that all of my efforts to control her "using" had not worked. Neither had hers.

What happened to my daughter? Where was she? When did I first see that she was lost to me—to her siblings, to her self? When did I first see that I was lost?

When did I first see?

I was along for the ride on the last hold of the rope in a game of "Crack-the-Whip." *I never did like that game.* And I sure as heck did not want to be in it now.

Recovery. Hers. She said she wanted to want it but she didn't. Until— *When was It?* She did.

Recovery. Mine. I rebelled. Held firm. It was about what I saw as my responsibility. It was about Love. Wasn't it?

Step 1: Why would I admit—*powerlessness?*

Step 2: Why would I believe I needed to be restored to sanity?

Step 3: Why would I ever turn my will over to . . . loving this child as I do? I'd like to see that plan first—take a good look at what God, Higher Power, has in mind for this child, and get back to this *God of Our Understanding,* later, when I'd had a good look at that plan. Where's the exception for the mother, in this powerlessness category? How can love like this be powerless in the face of what is most cherished? Why does the formula for *love* and *vulnerability* always seem to come to the same total: Vulnerability intersecting Love with a summation too big for us to hold by ourselves?

This much, *I admitted.* This much, *I came to believe.* This much, brought me to the only place of salvation—something more, than my will.

Eyebrows drawn down, I tap the numbers—calculating distance.

Why am I doing this? To have measure of these day-after-days, when all else was too amorphous to hold onto—when nothing was getting accomplished?

Except, the miraculous. Except redemption. Forgiveness. Grace.

. . . xx miles, times xx trips, times twice-per-day + the drive today, the last in this siege of driving, siege of gratitude. Numbers jump one-at-a-time onto the tiny screen, and total: One. Zero. Zero. Zero: 1000.

One thousand miles. Exact. I repeat the calculations—to truly admit, to come to, to make the decision, finally, to turn, to the care of . . .

I admitted, that all of my efforts . . .

I came to . . .

I opened, to caring from something greater . . .

I came to *Step One*

. . . came to believe that, sometimes

The journey of a single step begins with a thousand miles.

Regret

Poetry Honorable Mention

• David Eric Northington

Regret tastes like a gun barrel
cold hammered forged death
shoved deep inside your mouth
trembling with one finger curled around
the trigger remembering every failed
love job relationship like bullets in an
endless magazine stacked one brass
cartridge on top of another fighting
to be the first one fired

Exploring the New World

Poetry • Doris Lueth Stengel

Out for my daily walk, dog leash in one hand, four-legged cane in the other, I meet a young woman. She is wearing an orange T-shirt with FLORIDA printed in large white letters. Her mounded breasts loom like mountains above the flat expanse of the panhandle. Key West curves to the east just below her navel while the peninsulas of her legs stretch denim while waves of desire break over the shores of her thighs. In the gaudy color I taste sweet citric nectar, behold the sun perfect in its roundness, before it plunges into the Gulf. Like Ponce de Leon, I gaze at this mirage, this Fountain of Youth that makes me thirsty, makes an old man foolish again, until my dog pulls me back into reality.

Bully

Gordon Reinhart, eighth grader at Four Corners school, stood a head taller than Miss Bennett and half a body taller than us first graders. He'd mess our hair as he strode the aisle in his high-water overalls to his desk in the back row. There he'd throw one leg over the back of the seat, flop, and stretch his lanky legs ahead of his sister Prudence's desk in front of him. Out of fear, we pretended not to notice his mousy hair chopped from a kitchen haircut, not to cringe from his teenage body smell and pimpled cheeks, not to jump when he crossed his hands behind his head and cracked his knuckles.

"Give him a wide berth," Dad had said. "Don't cross him."

Mother, when we said our prayers at night, would add "and watch over the Reinhart children," then bury her face in her hands and nod her head, as if she knew a dark secret. We knew Mr. Reinhart had spent time in the loony bin, and Mrs. Reinhart had her share of nervous breakdowns. On those occasions, neighborhood men would milk the cows and haul hay; their wives would bake cakes and hot dishes, delivering them to the door but never stepping inside.

It was a warm September afternoon, and the kids, all from farm families, were less eager to learn than to relax after a summer of herding cows and cultivating corn. In the school yard during lunch hour, Prudence had found a garden snake swallowing a frog. As a science project, Miss Bennett lent her watch to Prudence and assigned her the task of taking notes on the snake's progress. At afternoon recess, her notes read: *One-thirty: frog one inch beyond jaws. One-forty: frog one and one-fourth inch beyond jaws.* The snake's progress was less interesting than Gordon's antics on the chain swing.

Gordon swung, pumping, pumping higher, yelling he'd loop the loop, pumping higher, higher, and yelling louder, louder. You couldn't look away. He was crazy enough to try it. Kids circled the swing, mouths open, hands holding their heads in disbelief, fear, anticipation. Then, in the nick of time, Miss Bennett rang the bell. Gordon jumped at the high point of his arc, landed like a string-less puppet and stumbled in behind us. Prudence stayed with the snake.

For the last class of the day, seventh and eighth grade literature, Miss Bennett called students to the front of the classroom with their faded red *Prose and Poetry* books. Gordon strode up the aisle, the small kids ducking, shifting to avoid him. Miss Bennett's procedure for teaching literature was to have students read aloud. The current story was "The Pit and the Pendulum." No homework was done by grades one through six during that reading.

Gordon stood to read. He held the book with one hand and tossed a pencil in the air with the other, always catching it. He began where the prisoner finds himself bound to a wooden bier with a surcingle. He stumbled over the word.

"Think of it as a belt," Miss Bennett said.

He read with glee about red-eyed rats swarming over the prisoner's body. And when he read "and their cold lips caught my own," first grader Sandra screamed.

Outside, a car approached, not Mr. Snyder's muffler-less truck across the road, but a car. Through the open windows came the yowl of chewing gravel, braking to a quick stop at the school, a car door slamming. Gordon stopped reading.

The rear door of the school opened. "Gordon, what's Pa doing here?" Prudence shuddered, waving her arms at the younger kids as if to tell them to take cover. "Gordon, Pa's here. Pa's here."

Gordon dropped his book and ducked to the floor behind Miss Bennett's desk. The front door crashed open and Mr. Reinhart marched in. "Where is she? She's coming with me." He wore a frayed straw hat, sleeveless shirt under bib overalls, and black rubber barn boots that came up to his knees. He was a tall man, with dark whiskers and bushy eyebrows that hid squinted eyes. "You." He pointed to Miss Bennett. "You're coming with me."

Miss Bennett must have known about Mr. Reinhart, must have been warned about him, must have been coached what to do if he confronted her. "Of course, Mr. Reinhart," she said with everyday coolness. "But I'll have to make a few preparations. Why don't you wait for me in the car?" She flicked her hand as if brushing away a fly. "Yes, wait for me in the car. I'll be there shortly."

When he walked out the door, the room was still.

"Gordon," Miss Bennett said, "run over to the Snyders and ask Mrs. Snyder to call the sheriff."

Gordon cowered. "He'll kill me." He folded into a tight ball under the desk. "He'll kill me."

"I'll go, Miss Bennett," Prudence said and bounded out the back door.

"Children," Miss Bennett said, "you are excused now. Leave by the back door. Stay out of sight of the car parked in front. Walk in the ditches until you're away from the school house. If you hear a car approach, run into the fields."

Gordon remained under the desk while students filed out the back door.

"Gordon," Miss Bennett said before the room emptied, "you may leave now too."

Gordon shook his head.

"I'll stay with you then," she said. "Don't worry. I'll stay with you." She reached down and placed her hand on his head. As the last of us students left, Gordon unfolded and stood, leaning on Miss Bennett, a pine tree leaning on a sapling, shivering, shaking, weeping. She patted his back. "It's okay, Gordon. It's okay. I'll stay with you."

He must have stayed. Mrs. Bennett must have stayed with him. Halfway home, a siren wailed from far, far away on the road to the County Seat. Louder now, louder and closer. Miss Bennett would hear it. Gordon would hear it. Mr. Reinhart too.

Change

Poetry • Larry Schug

A speaker at a seminar said
that in these uncertain times of Bottom Line
how rare is upward mobility,
you're lucky if you have lateral stability.
A person needs to be prepared to change, he said;
jobs, even careers, at any time,
change houses, change towns,
change states or countries or continents
four or five times or more
during a working lifetime,
you know, like we change underwear,
cars, bars, waistlines, hairlines,
medications, dedications, wars and whores,
like we change husbands and wives,
even sons and daughters.
My mother told me more than once,
"You'd better change your tune, Mister."

Broken

Poetry • Sonja Kosler

He makes promises
to the woman who perceives
him a tyrant, the keeper.
As she degenerates, deteriorates on
Mr. Alzheimer's playground,

he waivers between reality
and vows made to care for her
forever.

Mindful of the words
for richer, for poorer
for better, for worse
in sickness and in health.

Why not in health and in sickness?

This morning she packed
for the European tour. All her clothes—
blouses, skirts, pants, dresses, underwear—
precision folded into the best blue suitcase.

He finds her
dragging that thing
down the block
past the grocery, the drug store.

She is unclothed,
green terry cloth slippers on her feet.

Promises snap, disintegrate.

Goodnight, Irene

Creative Nonfiction • Audrae Gruber

Pushing the white metal button next to the large oak door brought footsteps and a solemn-looking man dressed in black.

"What do you want?" He frowned as he looked down at me.

"I came to see my friend Irene."

"Visiting hours are over." Then, looking around, he said, "Are you alone?"

I nodded, standing as straight and tall as I could, a little breathless. It was a hot summer day and I had run the two blocks from home.

"All right, follow me," he said, with one of those looks grownups get when annoyed and interrupted. Without a word, he led me to a room at the back of the building and left, closing the door behind him.

The room was large and cold and dimly lit—bare except for the strange wooden bed at one end with someone in it and a sign nearby which said, "Irene Salkin." It didn't look like my friend, but as I cautiously walked around it, I saw the mole on her cheek and decided it must be. She looked like a sleeping princess but older and had make-up on her face. She was wrapped in a white blanket with only her hands and head showing. I thought of the stories about the prince and the princess and how what seemed like death in the story was changed when the prince arrived. I had even seen a newspaper article about such a thing happening—that someone seemingly dead was not really. Surely, this must be one of those mistakes.

"Wake up, Irene, it's me," I said softly, so as not to disturb the man in black. No response.

I wanted to touch her hand but was afraid that would leave a mark or something and people would know and maybe that was not allowed. I did it anyway, very gently. Her hand was cold and felt like one of my soft white gloves I wore to church. I sat in the large wooden chair next to the casket and thought about Irene. She had been very sick with a fever and even in the hospital. When she was home, I went to her bedroom window to talk and wave at her. I wasn't allowed to go in because my mother thought I would catch something. I never thought she would die. Only old people died, like my grandmother last year.

Irene was thirteen and a couple of years older than I was. We were the only two girls on our block. All the other families had boys—lots of boys all ages. She liked doing things outside like I did. We collected pretty weeds in the empty lot next to her house, rode our bikes, played jacks and jump-roped, went sledding in the winter, played softball in the street with the neighborhood. Going to Saturday matinees on a Saturday, we would put on orange lipstick. Took it off before we left so our mothers wouldn't see. Fun pretending.

Irene, her mother and older brother Sonny lived just a few houses away. Her mother sewed for a living and even made us matching sunsuits—a kind of shorts with a bib top. But Irene had to stop wearing hers. One day the neighborhood boys had tried to pull her shoulder straps down and she ran away. When we asked her brother Sonny why they would act that way, he told us that boys did things like that—made no sense to us.

I sat next to Irene for a very long time thinking. I felt badly that I hadn't had a chance to see her and tell her how sorry I was and that I didn't want her to die. The cold air gave me shivers; at least I thought it was the cold air. Taking one last look, I tiptoed out through the maze of closed doors, shutting the big oak door carefully so as not to disturb the man in black. The warm sunshine felt good. Everything looked the same as when I went in but somehow it didn't feel the same. The image of Irene in that lonely, cold, dark room never left me.

"How did it go?" asked my mother's voice from the kitchen.

"Fine," I said in my most convincing voice, avoiding discussion. I went upstairs to my room. My eleven-year-old mind filled with questions. How did this happen? Why did someone so young die? What was death?

Questions I still try to answer—seventy years later.

Memories   Poetry • Annaliese Gehres

creak like floorboards
groans from the past
distant footsteps
tiptoeing through daylight
stomping across my dreams.
They are that tickly stirring inside
the best and worst emotions
sometimes running down hallways
or bathing me in sun.

No Pups Born to Isle Royale Wolves

Poetry • Barbara Draper

APNewsBreak. March 25, 2013

There was last year—
the alpha male and female and one more,
plummeting down a snow-covered abandoned well,
a "so sorry" unintended consequence of man.
It was a year before they were found,
broken, at the bottom of the well.
Only a shard of moonlight touched them—
not enough to reignite the light in their eyes.
Not enough for the man-in-the-moon to spit
in the mud and swirl it around
to create a new pup.

For the remaining eight—
no soft fur to nuzzle, no playful tussles,
only the cold wind
ruffling your thick gray coat, as you howl
out over the ice of Lake Superior.

So now you wait, on an island in a lake,
in a country, on a continent on earth,
like the last tribe standing
after another unintended consequence,
waiting with the moon,
for the night when there will be
no more vespers.

Like a Cat

Poetry • Colin Murphy

A thought like a cat
Unfurls from my heart
And stretches on a page
And yawns—tongue curled.
It unfurls in squiggles
And lines, in bumps
And swirls—and
Softly pads away.

What is it about the middle

Poetry • Sandra Sidman Larson

that makes it so
Midwestern?
Wind from
all directions?
Nothing
to stop it?
No balance
necessary; it lies
flat. Here
everything stands out.

My North Woods Persona
Creative Nonfiction Honorable Mention

• Mike Lein

I hurried into the small town lumber yard while oldest son Andy and Kaliber, the ever present black Labrador retriever, waited in the pickup. My list was short and so was my patience. But things don't move too fast in small towns on late summer Saturday mornings. A middle-aged couple was ahead of me, making small talk with the clerk while checking lumber prices for a home addition. I willed myself to slow down and lurked in the background until they finished and left the harried-looking clerk to deal with me.

"I just need a couple treated 4x4s—twelve footers," I told him.

"Man, I don't know," he said, worriedly checking inventory on the computer. "We're waiting for a new shipment. The ones we have left are pretty scabby." He looked up, expecting trouble.

"No problem," I replied. "I don't need good stuff. I'm building deer stands with a chainsaw."

That made him happy. "Great! I'll discount them. I love people like you!"

I heard a quiet laugh and looked behind to see a new customer. He looked like he knew all about chainsaws and deer stands. All six and a half feet and maybe three hundred pounds were clothed in shoulder-length gray hair, a half-buttoned flannel shirt, and bib overalls with a nice patina. In spite of this rough look, my first impression was that he likely had a part-time job as Santa Claus during the holidays.

I smiled back and walked out, chuckling at the note printed on the invoice—"UGLY!!!!! Deer stand material!!!!"

Andy was waiting, ready with a comment. "Did you meet Paul Bunyan?"

He was right. The cheerful giant in the store could be the great grandson of Paul Bunyan. Then Andy pointed to the right. "Look at his truck."

There sat the modern day version of Babe the Blue Ox—a 1980ish Ford flatbed painted green and rust. Spare chainsaw chains hung in the interior of this old girl and her bed was piled with gas cans, chainsaws, and a mostly empty case of Bud Lite.

I couldn't help feeling a bit jealous as we loaded the crooked posts and headed out. I had a better truck and my oldest son and a well-bred dog for companions. But this guy had life figured out. I bet everyone in town knew the gentle giant in the old truck. He was a man sure to be noticed and remembered. In contrast, I was well over half a century old and still struggling with my identity.

I don't have the money or the fancy log cabin needed to be the "Rich Guy from the Cities." I have thought about trying the "quirky environmentalist with the long hair and pony tail" thing but my spouse Marcie would probably nix the long hair even though I had it back in college. I also don't have the build to pull off the Paul Bunyan logger look and Marcie would not go for the bib overalls either despite the fact that she used to wear them back in those college days.

These thoughts kept with me throughout the deer stand building and into the next morning at the cabin. While everyone else snoozed, the dog and I wandered down to the dock and fired up the little boat. Late summer is not the best time to fish Crooked Lake. The crappies have long since left the shallows and the bigger northern pike have likewise retreated to depths unknown. But a full mug of coffee, a fishing rod, a boat, and a dog make a good combination on a lazy summer morning and there's always hope when you're fishing.

We headed east down the shore of Road Runner Island, trolling just outside of the oval-leafed pond weeds. I cut the motor at the south tip of the island and drifted across to Stony Point, casting into the lily pads. A bass smacked the lure, dove deep into the weeds, and freed itself. After that quick excitement, there was nothing except a silly little northern pike that missed the frog-colored lure, arched out of the water like a dolphin, and made me laugh out loud.

One other boat was visible, a classic red and white Lund like mine, drifting along Big Island. I didn't recognize it or the lone angler casting towards shore with a push button reel. I waved as we drifted close. Kal stood on the gunwale, tail wagging, eager to meet a new friend.

"How's fishing?" I called over.

An elderly man, well into his seventies, smiled back out the hood of his sweatshirt. "Oh, not too bad. Haven't caught anything but I had a couple nice bass on."

"Same with me—lost a nice one back there by the point."

"Well, that's fishing," he replied. "It's still nice being out here on a beautiful morning on a beautiful lake. Too bad I got to head home."

As he fired up his motor and cruised back towards the boat landing, a stereotype came to mind. I'm willing to bet there was something like a ten-year-old pickup parked back at the access, shiny, clean, and looking like it just rolled off the show room floor. Somewhere back in town, in a cozy home, was a gray-haired grandmother, baking cookies, waiting for her husband to return.

Kal wagged her tail, watching like an old friend was leaving. That's when it dawned that I might have just seen me, a quarter of a century from now. Not a rich guy with a fancy boat. Not an old hippy with gray hair pulled back into a pony tail. Not an aged Paul Bunyan wannabe in bibs. Just some quiet old guy, happy to be fishing on one more summer day.

So maybe that's the future. And maybe that's not so bad. But I wonder, maybe, if I could at least have a black dog in the boat?

Grief

Death should be expected when you are ninety-two.
Still, the weight of it,
like the blood-orange sheen of sunset casting a pall over the frozen
      lake.

Out the window, all is quiet,
the illusion of winter, I think.

Soon the temperature will plummet,
a late evening jay will shriek, fighting for the last seed at the feeder,
snow machines will drone on a distant trail,
ice will contract with its low murmuring groan.

Fish houses will light up,
scattered luminaries filled with winter warriors
whose blood runs thicker than mine,
embracing the cold.

I imagine dark forms bundled in down jackets and fur-lined hats
hunkered beside augered openings in ice,
dangling green-neon jigs into tangled weed beds below.

Out there a large-mouth bass will flop wildly
over the hard-packed surface
in its struggle to be free.

Perhaps tonight, one angler, rejoicing solely in the catch,
will ply the shanked hook from its bloodied lip,
release it gently back into the slush-filled hole.

Outside the Sunflower Market in Boulder, Colorado—July

Poetry • Kevin Zepper

The young woman wears blue and white snowflake pajama pants and a pink fun-fur sweater. She lugs two eco-green market bags full of groceries. Oranges and bananas are heaped on top of each bag, ready to spill with each small footstep. I ask her if she needs any help with the heavy load. The woman glares at me with cat's eye marbles, filling onion lenses of her thick glasses. On tiptoes, she jumps back, clutching the grocery bags like threatened infants. *Sorry*, I say, and walk to the other side of the street. Moments later I hear a loud *shhh* sound in her direction. It's the girl with anime eyes, squishing her market bags tight. Her hiss is rhythmic, like a sweating water sprinkler. She warns me away with her constant *ssss . . . ssss . . . ssss . . .* After she turns the corner near 14th, the sound of steam dissipates, quieted further by the calming sycamores. I slither down the damp side street, whistling between my teeth and split tongue under boughs of alligator pines.

The Barn

Creative Nonfiction • Sharon Harris

I still come here frequently to this place, seeking a quiet refuge from the confusion of the outside world: my job, my own family, too many words echoing in my head. This summer, walking in the main level of the barn on the old home place, I looked up at the ceiling and I could see all the way up into the haymow. Those perfect rafters still arced up to the peak, but I should not have been able to see them from down on the main floor. I noticed more holes, more broken windows, more stains where water had run down from above. Openings yawned in the main floor's ceiling to match the holes in the roof. I could hear the wind blowing through the broken windows. Was the building trembling? I hurried outside.

Fifty years have passed since I was a child here. Today, the barn is still standing, but nothing is like it used to be. The weight of the old building has popped out most of the glass in the windows. Some of the outer doors won't shut right. During every windstorm, shingles flutter down onto the lawn. Bare spaces have appeared on the barn roof. When we last ventured into the haymow, the ceiling high above us was checker-boarded with squares of daylight. We noticed wet spots on the haymow floor, turning soft and black as the wood rotted.

I remember long Kool Aid-flavored summers, swinging in my rope swing, touching the sky with my toes. As I swung in my swing, I could see the cow pen, where the cows came back to drink when they returned from the pasture. Next to that was the huge barn, the heart of the farm. We had the old style barn with the hayloft above it. Barn swallows darted after mosquitoes, returning to their nests of mud under the barn eaves.

Everything centered around the barn. We were constantly busy with chores in the barn or we were bringing hay bales or corn shocks back to the barn. We took the cows out to pasture and brought them back to be fed and milked. My sister and I fed the calves and cleaned their pens. Dad cleaned the barn and fed silage and hay. My sister and I played in the haymow, swinging from the old ropes, inventing games. The barn housed the cows where Dad and Mother milked them and raised calves from them—it was their life, how they made money and how we all lived. The huge structure was a refuge, absolute safety; it symbolized our whole way of life. We knew it would stand strong forever.

In the summers, we also helped Dad bring in the hay bales from the hayfield. We always wanted to be the one to drive the tractor, sitting up high in the cool moving air—much more pleasant than sweating, stacking bales on the wagon as Dad threw them on. When the wagon was full, we would ride on top as Dad drove back to the barn. Then came the job of getting the hay bales up into the haymow. Dad would park the wagon close to the barn where the red elevator reached down from the haymow door. He and one of us went up to the haymow to catch the bales from the top of the elevator and stack them. Now we wanted to be the one on the wagon, putting bales on the elevator, out in the air. Up in the haymow, each breath you took was heavy with swirling dust, weighing down your lungs.

One good thing about working up in the mow was just looking at the sheer size of the barn. The rafters reached up forever. I would stand in the middle of the haymow and gaze upwards. How on earth could simple people, fifty to a hundred years ago, build such a structure? To me, it was like building the pyramids. How did they lift these rafters up and fasten them? Heck, how did they even build them? The rafters curved high on each side of the mow, way up to where they met at the peak. In our young lives, these miraculous reaching rafters proved anything was possible.

I have not dared, now, to go back in. This huge unchangeable shelter from my childhood has become something I fear, a danger to unsuspecting grandchildren, a danger to all of us. I feel exposed and lost. My sister owns it; I have no say in its future. If I was rich, I would reshingle it, fix the roof and the haymow floor, preserve it, keep it as my shelter and protector. Oh, I dread the end of it, the thought of it collapsing or being torn down by unfeeling hands. But if I am afraid of it, with my love of its history, then the rest of the family is more afraid of it. I know I will not be able to watch it going away. I only hope that there will be some comfort, eventually, in seeing a new piece of open sky behind it when it is gone—a piece of sky, a stretch of trees, a hint of a future that we have never noticed before.

Twilight Crossing

For Jerry Schmidt (5/31/1955 – 9/23/2013)

Poetry Honorable Mention

• Thomas C Stetzler

Quietly you completed
your earthly works,
saddled the black gelding
and rode hard
down that last rugged mile.

I can scarcely take it in—
the thought of you
safely across the Jordan
in the Promised Land
smiling serenely,
the lathered gelding
returned to the barn
without you.

The Bait Dealer

Poetry • Gene R Stark

Selling fun, sending happy faces to the sun,
Answering the repetitious question for the hundredth time that day:
"Fish biting?"
What can he say
But, "Some are catching; need some bait?"
"What they bitin' on; better early or late?"
"Crawlers, leeches; morning, evening; deep during the day."
Optimistic, full of hope, they drive away.
For they have consulted the prophet of the thermocline,
The sage and sober master of the slime,
Broker of minnow-hordes and planer-boards.
The Bait Man is the keeper of the secrets of the deepest lore,
Though he hasn't wet a line in a year or more.
He knows what he needs to know
To make the business go.
He knows the inventory of stick-bait cranks,
And how many sucker-minnows inhabit his tanks.
He knows what advice will help to sell the bait above his cost,
To even out the over-stock and sell the worms before they're tossed.

The Great Minnesota Winter Commute

Poetry • Heidi Hemmer

I. The Car Commuter

A dead snowman covers your windshield. You don't slip on the mittens your mother gave you; you are tough. You put the key in the ignition, while you scrape the car. Sitting out in negative six degree weather, Mr. Dodge shudders and moans. The dark morning reminds you how much you miss summer. You drive down I-94. There has been an accident. Why is it that no one knows how to drive in winter, but you? Cars try to budge, but you are riding bumper to bumper. Not even the hillbilly pickup truck from Cottage Grove bothers you. You arrive to work forty-five minutes late. You take off your slushy boots and slip into your heels. You put your brown-bagged lunch away in the bipolar fridge (sometimes it freezes your soda, sometimes it melts your Lean Cuisine). You reach into your bag for your laptop (all the work you did over the weekend) and realize it is not there.

II. The Bus Commuter

At six below, you wait at the bus stop for the 4P to downtown. The usual three wait with you: the guy with the long pony tail who enjoys comics, the blonde with curly hair who you see everywhere but never acknowledges you or says hi, and the emo punk teenager who always lights a cigarette and smokes it in a depressing way. The cold air attacks your nostrils, freezing the hair, making your nose run. You push up your scarf to cover your nose and mouth, but then it fogs your glasses. You walk back and forth in a circle, just so you can feel something. You look down the road for the 4P, 4P, 4P, 4P. The bus crawls stop by stop. The roads are bad. The traffic is bad and there has been a bad accident. Forty-five minutes late, you take off your slushy boots and slip into your heels. You put your lunch away in the bipolar fridge (sometimes it freezes your soda, sometimes it melts your Lean Cuisine). You reach into your bag for your laptop and realize it is not there.

9 Below It's Cold

Poetry • Becky Liestman

Washing dishes in Minneapolis I disappear
into Texas. Long lazy laughing nights at Artz
in Austin smell sweet like
barbeque smoke.   Yellowed ceiling
tiles look down, tell the story
of all the partying & good times.
Sweet fiddles   sing bluegrass.
Later we meet at Donn's Depot on 5th
the sagging plush of train car, that old bar
and ten thousand gig stage
is a piano-pounding guitar-swinging song.
Let 'er Rip sucks us in,
grabs the dancers two-stepping   on the old time
wood floor.   Those cowboy boots
shuffle & clack I ain't gonna die.
So I say, Let it fly!

Lost in Windows 8

Creative Nonfiction • Cindy Fox

A devoted Windows XP user for more than a decade, I felt like I was losing my best friend when I heard my computer's operating system was being phased out. My refurbished Dell computer stored all the stories I'd created since I started writing five years ago. Stories I could never recreate with my fading memory. While Windows XP wheezed on unattended life support, my computer slowed to a crawl like an old woman who had lost her cane. I knew Dell was sick when an angry red shield with white crossbones popped on her face and wouldn't go away: "Your computer might be at risk!" At that moment I knew why my anti-virus program was free.

After paying a PC fix-it man $150 to deworm Dell and replace her dying battery, which took two weeks to dig out of a warehouse that stored obsolete parts, he retrieved my stories. When he said Dell's memory was almost full, my elation deflated like a pin-pricked balloon. And when he asked if I used a backup system to save my work, five years flashed before my eyes. What? After a severe sermon I felt like I'd been living on the edge for trusting free anti-virus to keep Dell safe from a computer crash. I took his advice seriously. I dropped Dell at home and drove to OfficeMax to buy a new computer and an external hard drive.

Back home I hooked up my new HP Pavilion and frantically searched for an instruction manual. A one-page foldout with setup instructions outlined a crash course for navigating the screen with "touch-friendly" tiles. What? I was always told not to touch the screen. No familiar start screen, no desktop, no programs. I felt like a goldfish in an aquarium without any water.

At the bottom of the box, a 13-page Windows 8 Basics guide provided all the information any smartphone person already knew. But, here in the middle of the woods where I live, cell phone towers are unable to reach the crevice in the earth we call home. No, I don't use a smartphone, but my cell is tucked in my pocket when I venture into town, only because I may need to call for help if I drive into a ditch after trying to avoid hitting a deer that's licking salt off the road.

After hours screaming at my notebook that wouldn't talk back, I resorted to touching her and accidentally bumped into valuable information: "apps" were programs, "charms" were settings, and "swiping" replaced the comfortable mouse I held in the palm of my hand. With false bravado, I opened the photo app, praying I wouldn't be paying for something I didn't want for the rest of my life. A photo loomed, filling the screen. But how do I make it go away? Where's the "X" in the corner? I swiped until my blood began to boil. My fingers fluttered like a bird with a broken wing when I unintentionally grazed the Windows key on the bottom of the keyboard and my apps came back. But where did my photo go? Did I delete it? Only Windows knows.

Enough of that. Writing deadlines, only weeks away, forced me back to my writing, which had been on a three-week hiatus. I plugged in my external hard drive and transferred my Word 2003 documents into my computer without a hitch. I opened Word 2013 the lady at OfficeMax had loaded for me along with the most expensive anti-virus program available. But this quirky Word version required my Microsoft ID and password. I remembered the nice lady telling me something about this. I dug into the box again and grasped a scrap of paper with my access codes, which made me feel like I was holding a winning Powerball ticket. After countless error messages, Microsoft confirmed my account was blocked after too many attempts to log in with erroneous passwords. I felt like they'd accused me of being a hacker. Well, that tipped me over the edge, and I howled like a baby with a dirty diaper.

I stuffed my anger inside me and called OfficeMax for help. They guided me on another unknown path that allowed me to reset my password. Lest I forget, I wrote my secret identity in bold-faced permanent marker on a huge piece of paper and taped it on the wall. So much for security, Microsoft. Now anyone who walks into my house can dig into my files and plagiarize my flowery words.

With the new Word task bar, I hunted for simple tasks that once were lined up in a row for easy execution. So many wasted days and wasted nights; I could strangle Bill Gates for hiring the techie who has made my life a living hell. I eyed the Word 2013 Tour, but I had no time to take a vacation from my writing. I navigated the tabs and drop down panes with "hit or miss" determination, knowing I always learned things the hard way.

While Windows 8 and I get to know each other better, I hope to master pinching and stretching, tapping, scrolling, dragging, and swiping which supposedly will make my life easier. But I do know my carpal tunnel will scream when I try my hand at the bodily functions of the new and easy Windows 8.

Lately, I get pop-ups for a free upgrade to Windows 8.1. Anything free now makes me feel leery. I'm tempted since this version has a Start button, which brings back fond memories of Windows XP. I'm already lost in the maze of Windows 8 and this button promises I will find my way back home. I hover over the download button, but something tells me to wait. I research the upgrade on the Internet, and for some reason this review doesn't surprise me: " . . . if you are already a dedicated Windows 8 hater, the new Windows 8.1 version will not change your mind."

One Thing, Beautiful, Every Day

Poetry • Kristin Laurel

Not the cruel winter wind that slaps the cheek.
Not the icy sidewalk that tries to break us.
During these grave days,
even when the sun is bright, it offers little heat.

It is late afternoon, and twenty-below.
My mother has been through many hard deaths,
she has every right to be bitter.
Instead, she says, *Find one thing, beautiful, every day.*
And stay in the present, daughter, stay in the present.
Right now, she's sitting at the kitchen table,
in seventh heaven and on cloud nine,
while she tells me of her new companion:

He's got a lively red mohawk, he wears a black scarf,
and he comes to visit her every day,
(most days, more than once).
When he comes to feed,
he makes her laugh, spilling seed all over the deck.
There is no one who loves him more than her.

I have seen my mother's cardinal.
He's wrapped in red ribbon, on a mound of fresh snow.
He doesn't sing, he whistles.
From the cold silence, whether by choice,
or by contrast, he reminds us,
even winter has a heart.

What Happens to Some Buried Things

Poetry • Sue Crouse

Spring, that gravedigger
who exhumes flowerbeds and fieldstones,
is late this year. The white berm

built all winter by the snow plow
still stands on either side
of the pot-holed road. I feel under-

ground, like the long-dead Swedes
in our cemetery—August, Karin, their daughter
Winnie next to my daughter Laura. My Love-in-a-Mist

is dormant, in the garden under the snow
and under that, the hearts of tiny tree frogs
are cold, yet still beat now and again.

Finally, a warm day and the drifts retreat
from the street and sink into the lawns.
Relics released from winter's tomb

are everywhere: a pink glove cupping
a lump of heaving lawn, an algebra test,
its equations scattered, squirrels,

not quite gone to bone. I pick up a Snickers bar
likely dropped from a plastic pumpkin last Halloween,
the brown wrapper still plump and crisp.

I tear it open and the package is empty—
faint scent of chocolate, golden stain of caramel
and a few pale peanuts, clustered in the dark.

Everlasting Light

Fiction • Susan Koefod

Edwina lay in her coffin and considered everlasting light. Given that she now had an eternity to think on such things, she took her time. Decades passed by in no blink of her eye—she could no longer blink—as she lay silently contemplating eternity.

Her subject matter was close at hand, inescapable, all that light glazing her in a patina of blessed permanence.

She did not want to cloud her thoughts by asking for her husband's opinion, which would have been simple to do, as he lay in the coffin right next to hers. What anniversary was it? Their hundredth? Or did the clock stop when he'd died sometime after their 56th anniversary? When she died a few months after what would have been their 75th?

She tried hard to remember, to count the moments, the birthdays, the silver and golden anniversaries. But it was getting harder and harder to bring it all back. She had memorized poems as a child, reciting them perfectly well into her 90s, but now she could only recall scattered fragments. She began to think of Emily Dickinson's "There's a certain Slant of light, Winter Afternoons that oppresses . . . " then lost the rest. What had that light oppressed? Then it came to her. " . . . Heavenly Hurt," and she realized then what it was about the heavenly light of the hereafter that bothered her so much.

She recalled a trip she and her husband, then newlyweds, had taken to witness a solar eclipse. They'd traveled several hundred miles to watch the moon occult the sun and observe a few moments of nether-worldly darkening.

She wanted to ask her husband what he remembered from that trip, perhaps now a century ago, or possibly a millennium? She didn't know exactly when it had been. Eternity expanded around her with no past and no future, unfolding in continuity, not keeping time by a calendar or a clock.

She decided not to ask him. She couldn't count on him to reconstruct *her* memories, anyway. He had his own to keep track of. It was up to her to remember, to dig under the layers of infinity gradually forgetting her entire life.

She remembered they drove all day and most of a night, slept on the hard floor of the van at a rest stop, making love inside the van even though she was both unnerved and thrilled by the flashes of light from passing cars. She was afraid they might be seen, yet delighted by the thrill of having her passion witnessed. The escapade made her bold enough, the next day, to initiate sex in broad daylight, when they'd parked in the river town where they planned to watch the eclipse.

He made her stop. She remembered him glancing out the window, a look of embarrassment reddening his face.

"No one cares," she'd said, hoping to change his mind. "No one will even notice," she added, though it was the thought of someone possibly noticing that made the idea so enticing.

"We don't want to miss the eclipse," he'd said, kissing her on the forehead and hurrying out. She bit her lip hard, tasted the metal in her blood. The light had already begun to dim, tinting the landscape in honey.

They stood on the riverbank, holding homemade contraptions over their eyes to shield them and allow them to see the moon as it swallowed the sun, the lunar mouth opening wide to taste a blood orange. The light thickened, went tawny then ochre, and even the birds went silent thinking that evening had arrived.

When the moon fully covered the blood-red sun, an orgasmic corona throbbed around them.

Minutes later the moon began to spit out the blood orange as if it had been too bitter, or too tangy, for its blander taste. Soon after, the sky brightened and the birds chirped again, as if nothing more than another morning had arrived.

They returned to the van, and Edwina remembered thinking she might try again. Had she? She couldn't remember. In the steady light of infinity, she could no longer remember the fleeting moments of her life: the sharp taste of a blood orange, the wet exploration of a first kiss, and even the momentary disappointments of love. All of the transitory moments she knew as her life on Earth were fading.

And that was exactly what she missed: those brief pleasures and painful disappointments that made you who you were, that told you who you loved.

She thought of asking her husband whether he still loved her. Did she still love him? They had promised to love each other for eternity, but eternity had not agreed to a bargain they had made on Earth. She lay, bathed forever in light, longing for love.

Wrapped in an Infant's Skin

Poetry • Patrick Cabello Hansel

He lies on the table, his clean diaper
soft underneath, waiting for the pins

to be fastened. Father leaves just for a moment;
there is an unknown light in the room.

What does a ten-week old reach for?
A wind, softness, skin? His joy becomes

a turning, then rolling, then falling,
his skull on the unwashed floor, wrapped

in an infant's skin. His cry, one whistle
of the desert bird, unaccountable. His eyes,

rolled back and loosing. His future? Scalpels,
skull pins, strange beds in strange rooms,

nurses holding his body like bread. His name,
cut from the mouths of his parents

like the wrong tooth, bleeds through the air.

Black Ice

Poetry • Michael Thomas Ellis

Black ice, so quiet in its triumphs and
So invisible in its purpose
No garish colors or warning bellows
Like nature's bolder assassins.

Coldly, it awaits the coming of innocence
Or a distracted carelessness
Until fate's impatience ends and finally
One world slides out from under another.

In that first chance at salvation
We slam down hard, on principle
In a panic of overcorrection
But nature's rules are mysteries now.

Furiously, we pump for solutions or
If we are courser and less evolved
Just keep to the original instinct
In surrender to a programmed defense.

But dominion proves illusive as
The immutable slippage persists.
Where we've been begins to twist in the mirror
And the inflexible tipping begins.

Awakening, we find ourselves alone
On our backs, wounded, eyes ascendant
Reliving every turning of the wheel
In that most private hour of doubts

3 A.M.

Lake Walk with Poets

Creative Nonfiction • Laura L Hansen

So near to the interstate, the ring road that holds this mess of cities together, we step out of the conference center, that looming swale of gray concrete and blue glass, and step down the 72 steps to the Lake Walk below.

A mile and a half around the lake,
a few undisturbed acres of land,
a pocket patched onto an old coat,
a bit of warmth, a touch of hope.

Alan, in his eighties and recently widowed, joins the younger poets, his feet tap-dancing along the leaf-strewn path, his tassel hat bobbing. His eyes are fixed on young Keegan who breaks from the others at the sight of every fallen tree or snagged limb.

While Keegan assaults the woods and clambers up laddered trunks, we stop and read from *Mary Oliver's Selected Poems*. We read of lilies and skunk cabbage, equally beautiful, and muskrats. We take turns and at Alan's turn he chooses to recite a poem from Edna St. Vincent Millay, a favorite of his late wife Claire.

At select moments, our readings are accompanied by spontaneous bird song, at others by mysterious *cracklings* from the woods. It is as if this is a church and the lake has partnered with us in a responsive reading of the psalms.

Branches snap and fall, birds respond in nervous chatter, bits of brittle black bark pepper the path. We stop, watch, listen, read—heads bowed. Noticing this, unsure why we bow as if in prayer or mourning, I raise my eyes to the trees, to the striped awning of the sun-lit upper story. But Oliver's words are like a hymn, so I close my eyes and drop my head again.

As each reading ends, I open my eyes and am surprised to find we aren't kneeling, hands cupped and waiting for the benediction, for some stranger to step out of the duff and brush and place into each palm a wafer-thin leaf the color of sun.

Oak leaves, bleached as bones
spread out across the walking trail,
a host of snow angels,
a foreshadowing of seasons.

Instead, as we round the final bend, the lake green with life beside us, young Keegan stops and offers us his brand new poem of poison ivy and biting fish. Youth. Youth is the wafer he slips onto our waiting tongues.

Yellow Tree

Poetry • Jennifer Lundstrom Hernandez

Cerulean sky interrupted:
the surprising technicolor splash of
yellow-gold her tresses,
a bouffant with attitude.

She stands there, tree-hand on hip,
daring autumn to do its stuff.
For how can such vibrant color
be a harbinger of death?

Oh yes, the day will come (and soon)
when autumn winds whip her mane,
and those bright golden leaves start to fall,
one flutter-shower at a time.

But what about today?
Why, today her locks fairly glow
in the Indian summer sun,
an affirmation of glorious life.

Just Crazy About My Job

• Beth Diane Bradley

According to a popular quote by Albert Einstein, "The definition of insanity is doing the same thing over and over and expecting different results." If this is true, then everyone in my profession is certifiably insane.

To clarify, I am not in the business of banging my head against a wall, I'm a salesperson. But I don't blame you if you can't tell the difference between the two professions—I struggle with that myself some days.

Most salespeople are not criminally insane. But I do think in order to succeed at sales, it's necessary to be at least mildly delusional.

For the most part, I've enjoyed the work, because I like meeting people and getting to know them. And frankly, there aren't many professions that pay you to talk, go shopping, and bring people free coffee mugs.

If I believe in something, I can usually get excited about it. And in theory, if you share your passion with the prospect, they should beg you to sell them your product or service.

Here's my take on how to make a sale without being committed:

You start by calling a business and asking for the decision maker. If everything goes your way, the top dog will accept your call and set an appointment to discuss buying a ton of whatever you are selling.

As I said, it helps to be delusional.

In reality, you will have to leave a message—and wait a few days before trying again. They will never call you back.

When you finally catch Polly Prospect, she will agree to receive information on your product or service and say you may call her back in two weeks.

She'll throw you a bone—and you will be grateful.

Two weeks later, you will call her again. She won't be there, so you will go through the same process, with—oh, oh,—the same result. After several attempts, you will catch her in the office. But she will have lost the email with the information. She'll ask if you could please send it again. You'll say sure, not a problem.

When you finally connect with her, she will agree with you that your product or service is something she might someday consider buying—and then it will become your job to make someday happen sooner rather than later.

You will leave Polly a message, telling her the price will soon go up. She won't call back. You will contact her again to tell her you will soon run out of the specific thing she might someday want to buy. She won't call back then either. You'll send her an email telling her the competition has signed up, and it's time to get serious, but she still does not return your call.

It's time to move on to the next prospect. You call and get his voice mail—decide not to leave a message, and try back later. He's not there. You drop in to his store and find out he is never there.

Salespeople must be extremely optimistic. So you leave your card anyway.

Then someday finally arrives. Polly calls and asks why you never got back to her, and you very tactfully explain you have called her, but maybe she did not get your messages. Your finely honed salesperson's instinct has confirmed that she is now ready to buy.

You gleefully rush off to her office to sign her up, and then feel obligated to spend half your commission in her store on the way out. You won't care. You made the sale, seconds before the proverbial men in white coats arrived to claim their free coffee mugs and haul you away.

Autumn Flight

Poetry • John Harrington

Field by field, furrow by furrow
clump by clump, it looked as if the earth
itself was taking off and leaving.

Knot after knot flew stubble-low
over picked clean and gleaned farms.
Flocks ascended

like clouds from ponds and wetlands,
formed contrail-high chevrons,
headed toward warm winter waters.

Stragglers practiced training flights
over harvested fall-black fields;
used umber-shaded potholes for "touch and goes."

Most rose like burning prairie smoke,
drifted east toward the Mississippi,
then south to the Gulf.

They had wings and the urge to go.
I, I watched with roots in the land of snow.

Lust

Poetry • Susan McMillan

Sunwave of summer
within the maw of blackberry branch
the maw of my hand
mottled purple and red

I do not carry home
the bucket of berries I planned,
disappointment no fault of the bush
but all my own,

for I have no self-control
and have eaten with lust
the profit of my hours
all my life

I have lusted after the best
and easiest things—
bees' honey, breeze-borne scent
of sticky pine, sway

of sweet rockets, dew-moistened
mops of lilac blooms
I reap without labor.
My whole life

I would spend useless,
wander from godsend
to godsend, stroke stiff
brown brushes of cattails

circling the swamp,
smell-touch-salivate my way
each ripe day of this life, ever
only reaching and tasting.

I didn't stop to pray when I came upon him. I was tired of all of that. Instead, I yelled, "Oh my God, there's a Bald Eagle down here."

We were four women on horses riding the old trails of the Minnesota Valley, and it was the last nice day of the year. We were trying to live, trying to forget, trying to do whatever it is we were supposed to do after my sister's children died.

Our horses plowed down the sandy bank of the shallow river, and we rode closer and closer, until we were less than twenty feet away. He didn't startle. At first we thought he must be sick or have a broken wing. We reached for our phones. I couldn't see my screen, the sun was so bright, but we started snapping pictures anyway. My sister cried, "It's a sign from heaven, a message from my boys." My partner whispered, "It's Eagle Medicine." Mom said, "Oh, he's just tame, probably used to seeing people on horses around here."

We sat on our horses and watched him dip his white-feathered face into the river. When he resurfaced, he opened that great yellow beak and showed us a mouthful of muddy water. He jumped in and out of the water and onto a branch. When he was on top of that log, his mighty talons seemed awkward. His wings, too, seemed out of place, so wet and so heavy.

My heart was heavy, too. And I felt stuck in between two worlds. And I wanted to believe. What does it mean to see an eagle on a dead tree in the middle of a stream? I started to let my mind fly; after all, eagles fly higher than any other bird. Legends proclaim they can look directly into the sun. Surely this must be a godly moment for Zeus himself turned himself into an eagle. "Maybe he will leave us a feather," I thought. Even though I'm a white woman, even though it's illegal, I would have given it to my sister.

It is winter now. The lakes and streams have frozen over. There's no sign from an eagle around here, except for the blurry pictures on my phone. I write less, read more. Yet every now and then I find something like a feather in a poem. Everything has slowed. My words have lost their exhilaration. They can't capture that eagle, or that day, and I am starting to distrust my own epiphanic endings.

All I can say is that we were willing that day. Willing to be alive. We were tender and exposed, and our souls wanted to go down, but that eagle made us look up. We saw that eagle, and he saw us; we watched him shake the water from his feathers and take to the sky; he followed the river upstream, his wingspan became wide, as wide as the receding river; he banked to the left as his image faded into the sun. And then we rode on.

No Mail Today

Poetry • Sonja Kosler

one quarter-mile
path to the mailbox
past lake cottages
abandoned to cold

fresh snow holds
delicate glyphs
formed by passing
chickadee, rabbit, vole

a blank page
decorated at the edges
like a crafter's
stamping project

blue-shadow tracks
disturbed by my
boot prints
large, clumsy, alien
alone

Tuesday Night at the Triangle Bar

Creative Nonfiction • Celayne Jones

It's Tuesday night at the Triangle Bar.

Twilight settles amongst the old storefronts at the intersection of Cedar and Riverside Avenues in Minneapolis. The West Bank, fabled hangout of hippies and home to dimly lit bars where blues music escapes from instruments and slithers out propped-open doors with the cigarette smoke.

It's early May of 1975. My college friends Barbara and Carol have given me the gift of sophistication, introducing me to the blues and the bars they are played in. A couple years older than I, they've had time to find the best places to go. That's why we are at this bar, a brick wedge of a building in an intoxicating part of the city. They've also had time to make the acquaintance of some musicians. Barb has an on-again, off-again relationship with a bass player in one of the bands. She's in love. He calls her when he's got an open evening.

The Triangle has a Victorian bar of carved mahogany with a large beveled mirror running along its length. The floors of the place are wood, deeply scuffed, and satisfyingly worn. A biker leans against the bar. In cowboy hat and leather chaps, droopy mustache, equally drooping blonde hair, he stares into his shot glass. A woman with wavy dark hair that reaches her waist, wearing a paisley skirt that brushes the dirty floor and a buckskin, fringed vest swooshes to the bar and chats up the bartender. He, a haggard-looking man of indeterminate age with hollowed eyes and rolled up sleeves, nods in time to her words.

Barb, Carol and I perch at a small square table near the back of the bar, sipping our beers and waiting for the music to begin. The band is on the stage, tuning up. Wafts of chords, riffs of tunes float briefly and dissipate in the smoky air. Now they're ready. We sway to the steady beat of this black American music played by white boys. We dance, together or alone. This place is far away, spiritually, from the college bars, with glaring lighting and blasting Top 40 hits. No college boys on the make at the Triangle. We are grooving among the counterculture, young lives germinated at Woodstock and Watkins Glen.

Men come in, mostly saying nothing to us as we churn to the music. When the band breaks, we find ourselves with a couple on a tiny fenced patio. A joint, freely shared, makes the rounds of the battered picnic table. Not much is said. It's about savoring the moment, inhaling atmosphere along with the smoke. I suddenly know that this will be a place I remember, even in the unimaginable decades that will come.

The music starts up again. A long-haired guy in a jean jacket tells me Lamont Cranston will be here on the weekend. He walks to the bar, orders a drink and lights a cigarette. The cowboy still watches his shot glass intently, as if scrying our collective fates in the surface of the dark liquid. A group of three, two women and a man, sits at the other end of the bar, talking through the music but moving with it, too. They look like regulars.

The drinks are cheap, and not very good. We buy another round. Carried away by the rhythm and soul of the music, we dance, each of us immersed in a world of our own creating.

In too short a time, the music is done, our glasses empty. We trip into the spring night, exhilarated, giddy. The world is young, as are we. There will be many more nights like this. That is what we think.

Thirty Years of Grit
Equals One Pearl

Poetry • Charmaine Pappas Donovan

True, when we first met
I thought myself unsuitable as a mate.
I was just steering clear
of that farcical first marriage;

so many hair-pin turns and tolls
along *that* twisted turnpike
it seemed far better to travel
on back roads for a while.

You, too, were still reeling
from a marriage of inconvenience
that became even more inconvenient
two children and thirteen years later.

True, you were persistent in wooing me.
(Much later you confessed
your curiosity about
what was under my baggy clothes.)
I needed convincing
that it was safe to fall in love with you,
a nice man with two children.

I became a believer
after you built an entertainment center
with a table saw and some tools
while your kids slept on my waterbed.

We talked ourselves into each other's lives—
and arms. I loved listening to your laugh,
I still do, and looking into your gray-blue eyes.

I relished raising a family together,
even when I became an instant parent
as we reared your two children,
then adopted two more made in Korea.

Over the years, you grew on me,
and I realized that finally
I belonged to you, a man
who made me happy,
something I never expected to find
if I beat the bushes looking for a
   lifetime.

Unbridled

Poetry • Stephanie Brown

She is a sun goddess filly
shaking lemon glitter
grains from wild elflocks,
muzzle waggling like a bobble head.
She dances near bristle-backed
hay bales and rusted tractors.
Her legs
crease at the hock
then kick toward heaven.
Whinnies of liberty
escape with the breeze.

As I drive closer, my presence stifles
her fancy-free groove, slows her
to a common trot.
Just a horse now,
waiting to frolic. Idling
at the bend in the road,
I wait for her to show me abandon.
I need her to show me.

Driving away, I look
in my rearview mirror and see her
dance again.
Coral-tinted sundogs
remind me how distance
can allow others to shine.

Dreaming a Life Together

Poetry • James Bettendorf

Two weeks each summer you visited
your grandfather, the judge, no one paid attention

knowing you'd go home soon. You were a flower,
I was your hero, and we played games in the woods

across the gravel road from your grandfather's
near the red dynamite shed. We made leaf and stick

houses and dreamed about the time we could do more
than lie shyly on the grass looking up through the leaves

as the trees swayed, the sun's warmth captured
under the canopy of oaks and maples. I anticipated

your yearly visit and we made plans to attend
our high school dances when we got older.

I will drive to your city dressed
in a fine suit and take you
in your yellow dress to the dance
a corsage at your breast
a gold bracelet on your wrist. You will say
He's not from this town. I will say
She goes to a different school.
We dance in the dim glow
my hand lightly touches the top
of your hip, yours rests gently
on my shoulder. We hold hands,
walk back to the car, my heart pounds.

When the judge died unexpectedly
the dance became the dream.

The weekend you spent in jail

Poetry • Nicole Borg

I popped popcorn and watched
the latest Johnny Depp release (and

was disappointed). There was
a lightning storm that night and the dog

cowered behind the couch. I couldn't
talk her out. No one called all weekend.

I ate cereal for dinner and breakfast.
I tried not to think about where

you were, but occasionally wondered
what you were doing and if you were going

to make a habit of jail. When I
lay down in our too-big-for-one-person

bed, I couldn't sleep, picturing us—how
you'd take my hand on our walks by the river

or play guitar, singing "El Cuarto de Tula"
to me or on summer evenings on the porch,

how we'd sip our drinks in the silence.
In bed, I imagined the heaviness of your arm

around me, the sigh of your breath
on my neck, your warm-steady presence—

I thought of you as you were
and I wondered if I would stay.

Just to Be Sure

Fiction • Tarah L Wolff

I asked her, "Where is your heart?" and she pointed to a corner of her kitchen and said, "It's there—I figure another week might be enough." And it was there, in a splatter of bright red blood on the black and white linoleum. It was nearly ripped in two and every time it beat, the two folds fluttered like a coughing sea creature on dry land.

I was rather horrified. "Aren't you afraid the rodents will get it? Or the cat?"

She shrugged. "When the cat finally starts poking around at it, I'll put it back." She scratched her chest a little. "My dog keeps watch over it for me." And it was then that I noticed how she had made no effort to spare herself either and had simply ripped open her ribs to get it out of her. (You could see the outline of the poor jagged things beneath her turtleneck.) I wanted to ask her if it was sanitary, this leaving your heart on the kitchen floor to be watched by the family dog, but that was a stupid question—her heart was obviously ill and keeping it with her had clearly been the worst of her choices in dealing with the damned thing.

She said, "Sometimes you need to put your foot down—there's only so much a woman can take . . . you know." I nodded, sipping my tea, keeping an eye on the heart in the corner. I found myself holding my breath between every beat, as if I expected it to quit at any time, though I knew better. Hearts like hers tended to live forever (figuratively speaking) like the least likable of the relatives, always the last to die. I found myself wanting to go over and inspect it, even touch it a little, see what a heart like hers felt like.

I must have been staring at it a lot because she said, "Go ahead if you want. You can't hurt the fucking thing." So I approached it cautiously, peering at it. The dog joined me, a big mutt, who glared at me a bit until she told him I was to be trusted. It was then that the dog trotted over to the heart as though to show it to me. He licked it and grinned with wolf-like pride. She watched with a bemused smirk while I leaned over and watched the veins pulse and the heart beat. It had increased when the dog had touched it; now it slowed down to normal again. I found my heart tended to try to beat in time with it; I supposed that that was only natural. Now that I was close, I could also hear it. It didn't sound good—sickly, whimpery. She had spared nothing when she had ripped it out the other night. The arteries were all torn asunder and the break down the center was wicked looking.

She stood beside me and we proceeded to peer at it together, as though it were an alien of some kind.

"Can I be here when you put it back?"

She said, "I don't want to."

I said, "But you don't look good without it, you know. You look like shit . . . won't it feel good?"

She sighed and returned to the table and her tea, itching at her chest again. "Yes, it will and it will be good, and I will feel good again, I suppose." She was very pale. I poked it with one outstretched finger and it was what I expected: meaty feeling. I returned to my chair opposite her.

The dog carefully picked up her heart with his teeth, did a few circles in the middle of the kitchen, and laid down with it in his jaws. He held it with his front paws and proceeded to close his eyes and begin a very thoughtful cleaning process that looked as though it would take some time. She sat with her chin in her hand, every bone sticking out of her back and face, looking as though she had not slept in a week.

"Have you talked to him?" I asked.

She blinked as though she had fallen asleep. "Who? Oh. No. Not him. Without that thing, I can't even remember enough to tell you about it. I think his eyes were blue . . . "

I could have told her all about it (and none of it would have been good) but she wasn't the one who needed to be told. We both watched her dog very lovingly clean her heart. I found my stomach turning at the sight and had to look away.

She said, "Yes, it will feel good to have it back, kinda hard to live without . . . you know."

I nodded, and could only imagine.

She said, "I'm just gonna have to start over with that god damned thing again."

I feigned experience, saying, "Some hearts just take longer to learn some things . . . you know."

She sighed and nodded. "He came over yesterday."

I choked on my tea and stared at her. She looked my way and nodded, head still supported by her hand. Her chest had started bleeding a little and it was coming through the front of her gray turtleneck, little blooms of red. "He couldn't see it, my heart, there in the corner, and the dog took it to bed right away . . . anyway . . . I didn't really remember him."

I found I had absolutely no words to respond with. I sipped my tea.

She gasped at me; her hand landed on the table with a smack. I jumped. She said, "Did you know a heart can scream?"

I hid behind my tea cup, appalled. "It screams?"

She said, "Yes! It screamed for me to put it back . . . you know, so I could remember him . . . God, how it screamed." She shuddered and covered her face. "He couldn't hear it though . . . he left. I curled up in the bathtub and waited the fucker out. It screamed all night until a couple of hours ago . . . it must've lost its voice."

The dog looked up and wagged his tail. He panted and the heart between his paws looked a little better.

I gulped. "Or maybe it gave up."

She said, "I'm gonna leave it out a bit longer though . . . just to be sure."

Preparing for Dinner with Ann

Poetry • Vincent D O'Connor

Rinsing vegetables under an
apostrophe of cold
water
I cleave them
open like her
soft lips split
in preparation of
an evening's passion.

Shards of Heartbreak

Poetry • Margaret M Marty

Fragments of shattered glass,
jagged edges,
non-stop slivers of pain,
wounds forever open

When the pain you feel
belongs to someone else,
the jagged edges
of the shattered glass

pierce deeper, sharper,
because there is nothing
you can do or say
to make it go away

Fourteen Across

Poetry • Lorie Yourd

Hours ago, we had each
gone about our own business
out of sync, distant,
unable to find words
of easy exchange.
19 down, worried, stressed
24 down, former sweethearts (2 words)
2 down, no future ____ ____
9 across, give or take

I told you about a problem at work,
my dissatisfaction punctuating
every sentence.
You, reflecting the anxiety,
told me to resign—end of discussion.
You had nothing more to offer.

3 down, speedy
19 down, impervious to light
31 across, barely gets by
35 across, caught a glimpse

You held back worries of your own—
medical limbo, no man's land.
How could I expect you
to consider my situation?

4 down, causes jitters
40 down, fermented drink
32 down, high blood pressure
26 across, restrict food intake

At 2 a.m., I reach over, plucking the
folded newspaper from our quilt,
I'm surprised you aren't in bed.
A rectangle of light frames the door.
We meet in the hallway.

14 across, to counter one's partner
by moving towards and away.

Bad Luck Sings the Blues

Poetry • Adrian S Potter

A three ball in the side pocket that kicks out
without explanation, a car engine's lifeless grind

when it's twelve below outside, or the ill-fated
misplacement of a prize-winning lottery ticket—

evidence of my existence, without fanfare,
because nobody wants me hanging around

with nefarious intentions. Humanity will never praise
my presence or understand all that is lost is found,

in due time. No one heeds my warnings, or admits
when a failed big break was simply not meant to be.

All they see is probability's bare backside taunting them,
or the raised middle finger of diminished odds wagging

in their face. They watch as I dismantle foolproof plans
and sever knife-slim hopes, void the magic conjured

from the cracked hands of working men. They call me
vixen and imagine me scorned, vindictive and craving chaos,

ignoring how even I, the lovechild of chance and superstition,
am held hostage by destiny's deliberate design. People forget

the moments when makeshift prayers were actually answered,
how they thought I had finally changed, not knowing how deep

I bear the scars of blame. They loathe my arrival,
the flutter of my fingers fashioning their misfortune,

never imagining that if I could take the pain they feel
beneath their fragile skins, I would make it mine.

The Power of the Shoes

Fiction • Sandra Clough

The night John asked me to be his plus-one at a work party, I pulled out my *Wedding Dreams* scrapbook. It was fifteen years old and falling apart, but the pictures of whipped cream gowns and multi-tiered cakes with figurines on top triggered the same fantasies I had when I was twelve.

We'd gone out only a few times, and I could see that John had his quirks, but clearly he was solid and steady with a bright future.

He fit perfectly into my fantasies.

Meeting his colleagues and friends would be a huge step. If they liked me, maybe it would nudge John in the right direction.

I found the perfect dress—a little black number that was understated and sophisticated, all at the same time—like the one Audrey Hepburn wore in that movie I can never think of. The sexy, crazy-beautiful shoes, though, found me. Silver chrome, strappy platform sandals with stiletto heels. They practically leaped into my arms. Unfortunately, they cost almost as much as my rent.

John was an accountant, and I'd seen that he was *very* careful with his money. He would not have understood such an extravagance. I dithered for nearly an hour before remembering what a friend once told me: *Never underestimate the power of the shoes.*

They were an investment in my future.

When the doorbell rang the night of the party, I yelled for John to come in, then waited a few minutes to heighten his anticipation. As I made my entrance, I looked down at my sexy, crazy-beautiful shoes and willed them to do their magic.

He did a quick appraisal. His eyebrows raised a millimeter. Then he rushed me out the door so we could get a parking space and not have to use the valet.

Apparently, John cared nothing about fashion.

Still, if a parking space commanded more attention than those irresistible shoes, I'd better be sure he never found out what I'd paid for them. Otherwise, our relationship would be over faster than I could say Jimmy Choo.

We drove around the fancy downtown hotel twice before John conceded that he would have to let the valet park his car. He handed over his keys, begrudgingly, and I breathed a sigh of relief. Hoofing it in those heels would not have been pleasant.

Another valet opened my door. The eleven-year-old Mazda sat low and he gallantly held out his hand. I took it and swung my legs around, daintily planting one stilettoed foot, then the other, alighting smoothly. The young man grinned self-consciously and made a clumsy bow. I curtsied and smiled back. The magic had begun, although John was getting his parking stub tucked safely into his wallet and didn't notice.

We rode the escalator with several other couples and I was pleased to note some admiring glances coming my way. I tried to look oblivious, at the same time hoping John was paying attention.

Approaching the second floor, we heard animated conversation and laughter coming from the ballroom. It was mid-May and tax season was over, so of course the accountants were feeling festive. At least, most of them. John was immediately snagged by a short, balding man who peered up at me and stumbled through an apology, assuring me he would only talk shop for a few minutes.

Thrilled to see how important my boyfriend was, I said not to worry, I would just get a glass of wine.

Now, I hold my alcohol fairly well, but I will admit that my judgment has been impaired after . . . too much champagne, say . . . so I had decided to stick to red wine that evening. I don't actually like red wine all that much and I reckoned that would make it self-limiting.

Somehow, though, every time I sipped my way to the bottom of a glass, someone handed me another. I smiled and, mostly, just stood there—like an Academy Award nominee pausing to have her photo taken, with one very high-heeled foot planted ahead of and slightly across the other. (It's quite sexy. The opposite hip juts out just a bit, making the thighs look significantly thinner.)

I don't know how much time passed, but "a few minutes" turned into several glasses and I was feeling rather giddy. The occasional hors d'oeuvre, snatched from the tray of a passing waiter, was ever so tasty, but a cucumber slice with a dollop of cream cheese and a sprig of dill soaks up very little alcohol.

Finally, I saw John coming my way and unwound my legs, thinking that now he'd introduce me to his friends. Just then, however, dinner was announced—which was probably fortunate because I might have had a little trouble getting my words in the right order.

Booze always makes me hungry and I was ravenous. As best my blurry vision could make out, the small, scrolled menu at each place-setting promised a feast:

Asparagus spears drizzled with citrus-infused hollandaise
Cream of shiitake mushroom soup with shaved shallots
Hearts of romaine with blue-cheese crumbles and cherry balsamic

vinaigrette,
Chilean sea bass atop sun-dried tomato risotto
and, finally,
Vanilla bean flan with burnt sugar

The meal was every bit as delicious as I expected and I relished every morsel. The *three delightful wine pairings*, though, left me a bit sleepy and I nearly dozed off during the endless speeches celebrating the firm's banner year. But, at last, they were over. I gave myself a little shake, wanting to be alert for the after-dinner socializing.

Then, I saw the band setting up. John and I met when he asked me to dance at my friend's wedding. This was an omen, if ever I saw one.

I shooed him onto the dance floor and snuggled into his arms. My high heels made us fit perfectly and I was sure we were attracting some envious glances. We swayed side to side with a half dozen other couples to a dreamy rendition of "Unforgettable," which segued into "My Funny Valentine."

I could have stayed like that for hours but, catching everyone unawares, the quartet swung into "In the Mood." I shook my head vehemently when John gestured toward our table. It was one of my favorite songs and my pulse quickened along with the tempo. I felt giddy all over again.

John's moves were more than a little stodgy. I think he liked maintaining his stuffy-accountant image, but I had enough style for both of us and this was our chance to shine in front of his friends.

Maybe it was the wine, or maybe . . . it was the power of the shoes. Those stilettos made it easy to sashay around the dance floor, exaggerating every movement. Other couples began drifting back to their tables until there was just us and one other couple left—and they were mostly just watching us. I loved it. I knew I looked fabulous—the heels made my legs look and feel like they went on forever. And my dancing was spectacular—weren't people always telling me I could have gone professional?

As John's movements became smaller and slower, he became more of a prop than a partner and I remembered a comic routine I'd done in a high school dance recital. My partner, supposedly, couldn't keep up and I'd grabbed another. John was, unwittingly, playing his part perfectly. Before the only other guy still on the dance floor knew what happened, I'd snagged his hand and pulled him in. I vaguely noticed the stunned look on his face as I twirled an arm's length away, then spun myself back toward him.

My backside was supposed to end up nestled against his front side, but the poor sap knew nothing about real dancing. Our bodies didn't meld, the way they were supposed to. They collided, like a ball of soft mozzarella being hurled at a brick wall. There was no flexibility in his stance and his knees buckled. My feet tangled with his and, in an instant, there we were, in a heap on the floor.

Too bad I didn't break an ankle. If I had, I wouldn't have tried to get up. And, if I hadn't tried to get up, maybe . . . I wouldn't have puked on my shoes.

The next thing I remember is sitting in John's car in front of my apartment building. He reached into the back seat and thrust a paper bag into my arms.

I sat for a second, clutching my expensive, sexy, crazy-beautiful, *fouled* shoes, thinking he would get out and open my door, but John stared straight ahead.

I opened my own door and swung my legs around, planting one bare foot, then the other. I braced one hand on the dash and hoisted myself up and out of the bucket seat. Before I shut the door, though, I leaned in.

"No worries about my shoes . . . I got them on sale . . . do you think your friends liked me?"

This is Your Brain

Poetry • Janice Larson Braun

This is your brain yesterday.
It hums with joy
At seeing names and dates and equations.
It purrs when you toss it words
Like "synecdoche" and "metonymy."
It feeds on data.

This is your brain today.
It is plumper and grayer
And not so interested in details.
It wades through the shallows
Of names and dates
With barely a fleeting glance.
It hums only as it slides
Into the deep pool of meaning,
Reflection,
And understanding.
Ask it what happened in 1066,
And it will shrug
And point to some murky weed bed
Over its shoulder.
But if you want to hear it purr,
Ask it why we don't learn from the past.
Or better still,
Ask it why people are so afraid of love.

ten years without you

Poetry • Susan Perala-Dewey

on my morning bike to work a brisk October wind slaps my face
as I brace for the long season of short days

it's the kind of cold that stings and starts my left eye leaking
single drops drip down my cheek onto wet black pavement

these are what remain of the plugged tear duct I doctored after you died
applying hot pads and boiled eggs to relieve the swollen lump

today my grief lives elsewhere

like your cancer that morphed from colon to surgery to chemo
from lungs to radiation to hospice

my grief has moved on from tears to thick calloused skin to
moments of memory

today split wide open as my tires spit wet leaves
my rusty spokes spin cold salty raindrops.

The Plan

Fiction • Marlys Guimaraes

I am so tired. I wish I could just shut my mind off and sleep.

It's two o'clock in the morning and, once again, he's not home.

Let's see . . . my purse is by the door, car keys on top of it, shoes and coat on the red chair, ready. My car is unlocked. I have my jogging suit and socks on. Perfect. All I have to do is leap out of bed, dash for the door (that is, if I can get around him), slip into my shoes, grab my coat, purse and keys and run to the car. I can put my coat on later, after I am down the road a ways.

Maybe I should just put my coat in the car now. That way, he wouldn't see me grab my coat and get suspicious.

No. Nope. That won't work. He might drive up when I am going to the car and start yelling and well . . . you just don't know . . . better not risk it.

And I don't think I should dash for the door. That would alert him, too. I'd better wait until he goes into the kitchen to get a beer. But then, if he goes into the kitchen, he might see me come out of the bedroom.

I suppose I could leave some leftovers on a plate on the table. That way, if he sits down to eat, his back would be to the bedroom and I could slip by him unnoticed.

Wait—remember that time I left his supper on the table for him and I made the mistake of leaving my dirty plate on the table, too? Remember how he came home in the middle of the night and started screaming at me because I ate without him? I was so afraid. Why didn't I leave then? Of course, at that time, I didn't have a plan. No car, no shoes by the door, no place to go.

Oh God. I hear his car. It's running. Maybe he'll just pass out and asphyxiate himself. Then this will be over. Oh no, the car door slammed.

Be calm. Be still. Listen for cues. You've done this many times. You have a plan. You'll be fine. Stick to the plan and quit shaking, for crying out loud.

I hear footsteps. They sound uneven. I bet he's stumbling. Must be pretty drunk tonight. He's at the bedroom door. I can feel him looking at me. Remember the plan. Breathe, breathe heavy. Fake sleep. Don't move.

Whew. He's walking into the kitchen.

Keys by the door, shoes, coat, ready.

Finally. Quiet. I think he is on the couch. Oh, thank God.

Well, it's been a half an hour. I hear snores.

Okay, nice and easy. Slow, quiet steps. Ahh, there he is. Look at that crumpled, bloated body on the floor. Reeks like the bar he came from. There was a day when I would bring a blanket and pillow and gently cover him. Now? I could care less. I hope every bone in his body hurts tomorrow morning.

Someday, I'm gonna leave him.

The Visit

Poetry Honorable Mention

• Marlene Mattila Stoehr

Now and then attendants add to or subtract from
the semi-circle of wheelchairs ringing the television:
nursing home mathematics.
Off to one side a couple sits at a table.
He holds an empty coffee mug;
her hands are idle, folded. Both are silent.
One is surely a resident—but which?

We whisper Ruth's name
and are rewarded with a
luminous smile of recognition.
She suggests we go to a quiet corner—
there by the man and woman will be fine.
We chat.
Where had we been? Where had we stayed?
Who had we seen? What had we done?

An adept manager of illness and heartbreak,
Ruth is suffering her final affliction.
She has no tales of activity to counter our full lives.
My heart weeps as she states in an accepting tenor,
"Life ceases to exist here."

Mwhai

My name is Mwhai and I am alive. For the love of God, look at me. I am alive.

Early this morning two of the village boys delivered me on this makeshift stretcher of poles and deposited me, delirious with fever, on the ground by the clinic door. About an hour ago, the nurse arrived by bicycle and stepped over me on her way inside. I watched as her dusty blue-black feet passed over me.

I have been pestered by flies though the mid-morning. I am as thirsty as a lizard caught out on a patio wall. My tongue snaps out as if trying to catch flies, but there is no moisture in the air. Just this dust, this dust. It coats my eyes.

Something is oozing at my side, something thick, glottal. I've been punctured, left here, the doctors are inside. Why do they leave me here?

The villagers did what they could. Moved me here, moved my feverish hide to a place where the children wouldn't bear witness to my death. They knew the doctors wouldn't treat a second wife, nor a beggar, for I am both. Still, I am here, and I am yet alive.

The flesh on my bones is scant. It must not have taken much for them to carry me here. Small as they were, those boys, I am less. I am less, even, than the weight of the veil that once covered my eyes. The veil lost now, my eyes are a feast for the flies. I try to close them, but they are too dry.

The sun is at its full height now and my eyes are being seared. I want to turn away from it but am too weak. I hear dogs fighting rough-scrabble in the adjoining yard, birdsong from the edge of the near-dry reservoir, the clanking of the empty bucket coming up from the well. If the hand that pulls it would but bring me a drop, I know I could make it to evening. I wait for nightfall, dream of cool rain.

Like tanned leather now. My bones laid out on the pallet like kindling.

There is movement at the door. I feel the brush of starched white linen across my face. A day of someone else's stale sweat. Lord, there is enough liquid in her body to still sweat, the sweet thought. A metallic click, the squeak of tires. I am alone then. I am to be left here unattended, seeping, dying.

My name, I tell the flies, my ever-present companions, is Mwhai and I am alive. Not as alive as you with your buzzing need, your trickling black feet, your blue mirrored eyes, but I am alive.

I am—Mwhai—I tell the moon. I— am—Mwhai—I tell the clicking of the crickets. I—am—alive, I whisper in my dry-paper voice.

The doctors are coming.

If We Only Knew

Poetry • Larry Ellingson

It bloomed in my muscle and crept into my bone
It threw me and blew me into the unknown.
Veins pumped with poison, body bathed in rays
I'm afraid of the dark and I'm dreading the days.

But the minutes and seconds are sharp and are clear
Each beat is counted and each breath is dear.
Now small things are large things and large ones are small
And the mystery in the spaces is the greatest of all.

Diva in the Front Pew—
Hypocrite in the Back

Creative Nonfiction

• Niomi Rohn Phillips

Kaua'i, Hawaii, January, 2014

She sails down the center aisle, then slows near the front pews, moving in a leisurely dance, from one side of the aisle to the other. Beaming, arms extended, she leans into the pews, grasping the hands of her friends and the local congregants.

She's average—but only in height. She's lithe and shapely, from a lifetime of surfing and tennis and horseback riding in the mountains of the island. She wears an elegant, oh-so-simple, designer dress cut just above the knee to reveal her attractive, muscular legs, and she carries a small Gucci bag. Her shoulder-length, blond hair is pulled back under a wide-brimmed hat. She always wears a hat, the only woman hatted in the small church sanctuary. She always sits in front row center. Today, she puts an arm around a grandchild on each side. Her son is ushering this morning. Her daughter-in-law, a dark-haired beauty of island ethnicities—Japanese/Caucasian/Hawaiian—sits next to her in what is, apparently, the family pew.

In the church newsletter, I note *Mahalo a nui loa* for *kokua* (thank you very much for gifts) to the Diva and her husband for the Christmas tree and for the wreaths and for the plumeria lei decorating the sanctuary cross and . . . for cleaning the church. The church is packed every Sunday, but only sixty or seventy people are permanent members. On Saturdays, volunteers vacuum and dust.

Her husband sings in the choir, a small group of *Haoles* (whites) and Hawaiians, who face the congregation from the altar, and are accompanied by ukulele and guitar. They sing in the melodic words of the Hawaiian language: *Ho- 'o-nani ka Maku* (Glory be to the Father...); *Ho 'o-na-ni i ka Maku-a mau* (Praise God from Whom . . .).

This church on the island of Kaua'i was established in 1834 by American Christian Missionaries. The Diva's great-grandparents arrived ten years later, joining other missionaries to Christianize the heathen Hawaiians. The missionaries substituted their God for the multitude of Hawaiian gods, banned the lascivious hula, and clothed Hawaiian women in dresses patterned after nightgowns. The New Englanders' notion of modesty—covering the sinful nakedness from neck to toe. This, according to some stories, was the origin of the muumuu.

The Diva is a direct descendant of those missionaries to Hawaii who, innocently or not, purchased or were given pie-shaped parcels of Native Lands by the Hawaiian royalty. The slices consisted of a tip on the ocean, widening to tillable land, and extending into the mountains. Ocean for food from the sea, land to cultivate, mountains for shelter.

The missionaries' descendants became the sugar cane and pineapple plantation owners and the money-men and bankers on the Hawaiian Islands, whose last Queen, Liliu'okalani, was overthrown in a coup led by Caucasian businessmen. Liliu'okalani abdicated. With American troops in the harbor, she ceded her kingdom to the United States.

The Diva lives in a mansion with guest house on ocean's shore; the family stables their horses and grows taro in the fields. They ride in the lush mountains midst waterfalls and views of the Pacific otherwise inaccessible. I do so want to disdain and dislike her.

Her grandfather and his two brothers donated the present church building to the congregation. The church, which is on the State and National Historical Registers, keeps its doors open inviting visitors. And the tourists come—in a steady stream all day, every day. Some coordinate their visits with the Sunday morning service, packing the pews of the small church, a few to worship, most to check off the site on their island bucket list.

If you arrive at least a half hour before the service begins and sit in a pew at the back of the church, you can find peacefulness here. You can center yourself. Meditate. The arched, stained-glass windows on each side of the small, green church are open. A soft breeze carries breath of wild ginger and eucalyptus. A dove coos in the stillness of morning at the edge of the mountains.

As the first strings of the ukulele sound and the Kahu (pastor) comes to the altar, the tourists are still pushing in the main door. They jabber in stage whispers waving cameras, cell phones, and iPads aloft panning the tableau.

After the opening hymn, visitors are invited to stand and introduce themselves. They do. And they give competitive weather reports ad nauseum from Manitoba, Iowa, Michigan. "We left -20 degree temperatures . . . " "The high was eight degrees when I left home . . . " "We had a blizzard the day we left."

I would be mortified to call attention to myself. And, after all, I'm not a tourist. I live here . . . well . . . sort of . . . in the winter. Smug, I join in singing the hymns in Hawaiian, conscious of the curious glances of the tourists sitting beside me.

I try to concentrate on the sermon and the worship service. The picture-taking and chatter are especially annoying this Sunday honoring the first Hawaiian Christian, Henry 'Opukaha'ia. Keola Yakotake, a tall, large, imposing young man of Hawaiian-Japanese ancestry, blows a conch at the door and proceeds down the aisle to the altar. Three women with orchids in their hair, plumeria leis, and long, white robes dance a reverent hula. The tourists stand, obscuring my view with their photo-taking whatevers.

After the last notes of the final hymn, I pick up my purse, gather my white shawl from the pew and wrap it around my shoulders, before I slide out of the pew and into the aisle. Lingering. Waiting for the people from the front pews to move towards the door, and maybe a chance encounter with the Diva. She comes down the aisle. She recognizes me from past winters, grants me her warm smile, grasps my hand in her two. "Aloha, how nice to see you again." And I flush with pride in recognition by the royalty.

The Survivor

Poetry • Thomas C Stetzler

I watch Mom sitting with old friends
at the funeral, her best dress hidden
beneath a spotted coat.

Through the static of her hearing aid
she gleans scraps of conversation,
weaves them into her thoughts, leans
forward to read lips.

Still confused, she shuts off the
hearing aid and withdraws into solitude,
balancing heavy questions on the arch
of her brow, a finger worrying a loose
thread.

Shrines

I read an interesting article about the Day of the Dead and how some cultures use November 1 to create shrines to their dead relatives and pets. They spend time with the items, remembering and honoring the love that existed and still exists. A little bit like a wake—is what I thought. I also thought that it was an absolutely wonderful idea that resonated with me. I imagined gathering up photos of my two lost grandmas, two lost grandpas, lost dogs etc., and putting them around objects that were close to them. Thing of it is—I don't have any objects that were close to them. Trinkets (or anything that sits around and requires dusting while having absolutely no use) just aren't allowed in my life. So, no shrines for me.

Now that I've said that—I embarked on a journey this last summer in the form of furniture and not only was it one of the most gratifying things I've ever done, it was also one of the most healing. It was hot, I was exhausted, sweaty and filthy. In the beginning I felt overwhelmed (sixteen pieces of furniture were sitting there looking at me with an expiration date of whenever it decided to get below freezing outside) and I also felt very alone. I was going through some very large changes in my life when it came to the people around me. I had decided that being betrayed and lied to was not something I could put up with anymore. I lost many I had regarded as friends.

I went alone to my garage and the furniture that had been waiting for me.

Fury and tears took turns on me. But the longer I worked, the less I thought of those people, and the more I thought of the people I had lost. When my hands ran over each old piece, I was reminded more and more of how it had been touched a thousand times by someone that I loved. I began to think on it so much that it became a living breath. Each time I touched a piece of furniture, my grandma's or my grandpa's hand was right there, touching it with me from years ago. I saw my grandpa sitting in the rocking chair that I had just finished, enjoying the summer sunshine. My grandmas I saw tucking away trinkets in different dressers that I was working on. And they all said the same thing to my sad and disappointed heart—all things pass away and few things on this planet are worth being upset over.

They were all common sense folk. My current circumstances would have seemed so stupid and preposterous to any of them that they would have disregarded my trying to explain. They probably would not have even understood what on earth I was upset about. And with every effort I made, with every piece of furniture I resurrected, I felt my heart coming back around. Once an old phrase came to my mind from Dr. Seuss: "Those that matter don't mind and those that mind don't matter." No doubt pushed into my heart by the presence of those ghosts.

I found peace.

Maybe I'm not much of a shrine girl but in my bedroom now I have two night tables, two dressers, one hassock and a rocking chair (and that's just in my bedroom!), all once used by people that I have lost and love very much. Every day I touch them, I use them, and I love that they are still my grandparents' in my mind. Maybe I am a shrine girl after all—just in a different kind of way.

Tom's Farewell

Poetry • Anne M Jackson

Fine white feathers combed into place.
First make-up ever worn on your face.
Paper-thin skin no more to be bruised.
Veined able hands no more to be used.
Sweater vest straight, shirt neatly tucked in.
Sharply creased trousers, shoes of calfskin.

It doesn't feel normal, you looking so formal.
This isn't the you the rest of us knew.

After the luncheon of ham and Jell-O,
embraces and platitudes lame and mellow.
After your flag-draped casket rolls,
and in the winter sun it glows.
After we jump as the guns first shoot,
a flag is folded and men salute.
After the pastor has the last word,
and feet shuffle past, I'll do the absurd.

I'll set down the flowers and lift up the lid,
so you can rest peaceful and die as you lived.
I'll rumple your hair and wipe off your face.
Untuck one shirttail and one shoe unlace.
Roll up your shirt sleeves past your watch band.
Prop up a whiskey in one gnarled hand.
Speak your first name and kiss your cool cheek.
Think of the stories you'll not again speak.
Then take a deep breath, and lower the lid.
And go to my car, and cry like a kid.

Jude

Poetry • Kevin Zepper

I've washed my soul in "Hey Jude" after every funeral I've attended since my closest friend died, consolation in the words of a majestic pop song strung in a spinning disc across the universe, ever revolving. Paul sings "make it better" and the music wells up in me like a spring of light and life in my eyes. The golden rolling loop of lah-dah-dah-dah-dah-dah-dah repeating, joined with abbey horns and strings, percussive piano, welcome notes breaking the leaden, sorrow shackles on feet. Voices merge in this hymn and chorus as the melody regenerates, restoring notes to a seamless beginning. And the fade, the fade so gradual and grand, the slow procession of bright souls and the primal affirmation of "yeah, yeah, yeah, yeah, yeahs" illuminating the space in shadowed valleys, leading me beside cool, calm waters; for there is no cold coda for the finality of things. Yes, yes, I, once a lost cause, will find it in my heart and under my skin, the reaching of arms across, about, and above in exaltation of everything in the now and after, warm summers in the comfort of green pastures. Yes, I will make the pilgrimage, ghosts of my ancestors trailing in my even, humble walking wake. I follow the rods and staffs of sound, recalling the sterile sting of mine enemies, how the shoulder's burden lightens, the rising sun shines in my heart, making it better . . .

Leo and the Cows

Creative Nonfiction • Tim J Brennan

At the clang of a bell, or some other Pavlovian B. Taurus response, a typical dairy cow will cease grazing and proceed robotically at a given time to its everyday stall to await the reason for its existence. Cows can be milk productive for up to seven years. Leo, a dairy farmer for fifty-four years, once told me it took about two weeks to condition such behavior once a cow came of age. It takes our public school system eighteen years to achieve a similar goal. And even then, productivity is often in question. But that's a different story. We're here to talk about cows.

A barrel-chested man with fingers as thick as breakfast sausages, Leo told me that attending to his dairy herd twice-a-day for fifty-four years disciplined himself pretty well, also. He rued his milking career, and conversations with Leo tended to be sad and short discourses. He commented often during our Wednesday night bowling league together, without prompting, that most folks weren't much better off than the dairy cows. After missing another ten pin or the seven pin for the third time, Leo would turn, spit chaw into a Styrofoam cup, and remark how much those damn pins were like his cows: sassy, stubborn, and often self-centered but, unlike most people, each owning a different personality.

Leo installed six speakers in his dairy barn when he noticed milk production increased slightly during "Polka Hour," a local radio program airing daily at 5:30 a.m., which happened to coincide with the first milking. He swore that when a commercial aired, the cows acted downright obstinate until another polka two-stepped beneath the barn swallows' dancing swoops. In a low voice, Leo once told me a polka beat was surreal, almost narcotic, and many times he lost his own sense of time, not remembering if it was Tuesday or Thursday or even Saturday. He had to staple-gun a desktop calendar to the back of the service door and X-out the days. The hypnotic "oomph pah pah . . . oomph pah pah," the harmonious pendulum of sixty dairy cows' tails swishing in unison. Imagine this rural ballet repeated every morning and every evening, 365 days a year for fifty-four years.

To the day he died, if he ever heard a polka playing, even as background music, Leo broke into a cold sweat. Elevator or store music was the worst for him. Leo's wife Margaret told me once that after a grandson's wedding, Leo disappeared, only to be found in a stupor in twenty degrees below zero cold outside the American Legion dance hall after a particularly long version of "Beer Barrel Polka."

Leo died a few years ago. After he left the cows, he ended up being my apartment manager. After school, we'd sip beers on the porch and Leo and I would have conversations that never failed to include the word "cow" at some point. They consumed him. Literally. I think about him at the oddest times. At the downtown cafe. In the pew at church. Different places where I notice people going to the same booth or the same seat. The greeting card aisle of a drug store.

I used to bartend during my college days and I remember certain customers tended to come in and sit on the same stools. They played the same songs on the jukebox. Most came in at the same time of the day as they had yesterday and they all said hello to the folks who were already there in the same place they always were. A few turned downright obstinate when some poor new sucker happened to have his or her butt on their stool, but they settled down when I set their regular order down in front of them. I knew what they liked. Maybe that's why "Happy Hour" is always at the same time, no matter what drinking establishment you're talking about.

Monotony. Passivity. Systematic Learning. People have different names for what happens to them. Leo called it milking. Folks ask me if I get bored teaching the same things over and over again. I've been doing it for thirty-odd years now. I tell them that each year has different kids. Different kids equals different interpretations, different opinions. So . . . no. But there are times when I'm driving my lonely two-lane county highway to work at 6:30 in the morning, and I see cows moving in the fields toward their barn, and I will think about Leo and his cows and hope that the students follow their normal routine for the day. Keeps the noise down. I'm sure you understand.

Learning from the Crows

Poetry • Chet Corey

The crows are gathering
over the night's kill.

They are the smartest of birds—
more communal than man,
seldom alone.

And what they hunger for
they find.

So unlike
the boys on the block
who call a bent-pin of a woman
that old crow,

knowing nothing of her needs
or how she met another's . . .
nor of their own.

Little Dreamer

Poetry • Larry Schug

(for Leo)

Of what did you dream
your first dream
outside the womb
did you dream of yourself
floating
in a warm amniotic sea
the safety of darkness
or was your first dream
of this new light
where life is to be lived
did you dream of a cradle
of gentle hands sweet caresses
the softness of a breast
a mother's humming lullaby
tears warm as love
falling as a gentle rain
on your new land of skin

The Grand March

Creative Nonfiction Honorable Mention

• Andrea Taylor Langworthy

Right step. Left step. Right step. Left. Slowly, but surely, my husband and I make our way through life using the carefully choreographed routine that almost always gets us to and fro without a mishap.

Over the years, we have learned I must lead and he must adjust his gait to my ever-slowing one. We start out on the right foot at exactly the same time. As we go, I grip the handle of my cane tightly with my right hand. My left is held firmly by his right, our fingers laced together like the pink satin ribbons of a ballerina's toe shoe.

His job is to look straight ahead for people in too much of a hurry to notice or even care about us. Mine is to cast my eyes to the ground, watching for a wrinkle in the carpet, an area rug, the rubber mat with an upturned corner, a crack in the sidewalk or a pebble which will be like a boulder beneath my shoe.

When we need to go somewhere, I make a solo performance down the ramp in our attached garage, gripping the rails on both sides. At the bottom, my husband takes my hand. I pirouette slightly to the left, use a cardboard box that once housed a barstool as a touch stone and make my way to the side of our vehicle. My husband opens the door. I side-step to it, grab hold of the armrest, raise my left leg to the SUV's floor and sidle towards the seat. He stands behind me, his hands outstretched, ready to catch me if I lose my footing.

When we reach our destination, he comes around to open my door. I pivot in my seat, stretch my legs to the ground, stand up and steady myself with the door he has put within my reach. Turning to the right I face the rear passenger door, leaning against it as I might with a handsome new dance partner. My husband closes the front door, hands me my walking stick, takes hold of my other hand and we slowly sashay to our journey's destination.

The importance of being in step was never more evident than the day years ago when we were shopping at Macy's. A young mother pushing a jogging stroller shot out of nowhere and barreled towards us. Her head was turned downward as she jabbered to her child. My husband quickly steered us toward a rack of clothes just seconds before the woman whooshed past. On her heels was her husband with another baby in a jogger. He made a grand gesture of swerving away from us but said nothing.

We weren't so lucky outside the dentist's office last fall. Located at the end of a strip mall, there is a handicapped parking space right in front. The city has cut a scoop out of the sidewalk to label it "accessible" but it is an uphill climb. Instead of ascending in a straight line, we take it at an angle which means overshooting the door a bit. That day, when we reached the top, I made a slight adjustment to the left towards the door but neglected to signal my move. My husband bumped into the side of my foot. I lost my balance. My cane fell from my hand and I began my descent. With the grace of a ballroom dancer, he tightened his grip and dipped me slowly to the ground which lessened the impact.

With all this orchestration, one might think I had once been limber and coordinated. But no, when my Girl Scout troop worked on our square dancing badge, I was the one who turned left when it should have been right. The one who couldn't do-si-do and promenade like my cohorts. "Two left feet," my mother liked to tease.

To rectify the situation and teach us the art of gracefulness, Mom enrolled my sister and me in ballet classes at a local studio. When she learned the class was a half-hour of ballet and another of tap dancing, Mom was not happy.

"I didn't plan to have you clomping around in clodhopper shoes," she said, but after we begged, she let us stay in the class. Plié and barre became part of our vocabulary but so did shuffle, ball and change. Perhaps you can understand our mother's chagrin when our spring recital had no elegant ballet, only a stomping, tap dancing rendition of the Charleston.

Mom passed away a year before I was diagnosed with Inclusion Body Myositis, a muscle-wasting disease inherited from my father. She never knew I was having trouble walking up stairs and stepping up a curb. (Perhaps I didn't tell her for fear she would attribute it to my two left feet.)

When my hubby and I are in good form, as we two-step down the hall to a doctor's office or step gingerly into a hair salon, I often wish my mother was around to watch our performance. To see how smoothly we move through an obstacle-filled world.

She would, no doubt, give the credit to my husband. Mom always liked him. Steady and sure, he is the perfect partner to be hand-in-hand with me. I'm still no Ginger Rogers but he's become my Fred Astaire. Cue the music . . . right foot, left foot, right foot, left.

Celebration

Poetry Editor's Choice

• Marlys Guimaraes

Heat glides down spines pooling at waistbands, long-sleeved arms pump trombone slides, unison knees time each step, children strategize for treats, a mama wishes the baby wasn't quite so heavy, envies Daddy his place in the shade, sticky fingers of cotton candy smell sweet, horses poop in the street, but not the ones that go 'round and 'round near spinning wheels holding screaming teenagers upside down, that eye strangers with longing carrying red and white containers of deep fried doodles and doughnuts; sweethearts impress with short skirts and long handled hammers that pound to hit red targets in the sky so when I realized that Mother was dying, it hurt to know there was no fanfare, no hailing crowds cheering her on her way, no standing ovations, but of course, when she arrived at her destination, I bet there were choirs singing "Hail to the Queen," jiggling jesters, cheerleaders in blue uniforms with silver tassels doing leaps and flips, flying flags and banners and I bet Dad was in the center clapping loudest of all.

A Harvest Day

Poetry • Barbara Draper

Today is a harvest day—
blue sky, trace of a full moon,
a flick and a scamper up the side of a tree,
and no one yet has explained
how a dozen days can be barren
and the next a harvest day.

Oh, I do ask for them—
though I never quite know
what I am seeking when I ask:
vague prayers,
for a lift, a surprise,
for a bird cutting orange on the wing,
stout blossoms that wink.

Then pods burst open on a day like today,
and people close to me are suddenly
as dear as pimento trees.
The air has shifted:
a little seam that let me in,
and I will sit in it, on this bench,
smiling, a touch loony-looking,
and here, I'll slide over just a bit.

"The talking stick is a Native American tradition used to facilitate an orderly discussion. The stick is made of wood, decorated with feathers or fur, beads or paint, or a combination of all. Usually speakers are arranged in a talking circle and the stick is passed from hand to hand as the discussion progresses. It encourages all to speak and allows each person to speak without interruption. The talking stick brings all natural elements together to guide and direct the talking circle." —Anne Dunn

This year, we received over 300 submissions from 159 writers. The editorial board selected 91 poems, 23 creative nonfiction, and 15 fiction pieces from 94 writers for inclusion in this volume. Please submit again!

www.thetalkingstick.com
www.jackpinewriters.com

Contributors 2013

Without the following contributors, this Talking Stick would
not have been possible! Thank you to everyone!

Benefactors
Louise Bottrell
Lisa Phillips McCormick
Jerry Mevissen
Harlan and Marlene Stoehr

Special Friends/Single
Charmaine Pappas Donovan
Mike Lein

Good Friends/Couple
Joanne Cress & Luke Anderson

Friends/Couple
Amy Fish
Kathryn Kirmis Medellin
Niomi Rohn Phillips
Deb Schlueter

Good Friends/Single
Eric Chandler
Rhoda Jackson
Sonja Kosler
Margaret M Marty
Joanne Moren
Carmen Penick
Shasha C Porter
Bob Sullivan
Jill Torgerson
Bonnie West

Friends/Single
Peggy Trojan
LuAnne White

Author List

Lina Belar
James Bettendorf
Sreekanth Bhaskaran
Nicole Borg
Beth Diane Bradley
Janice Larson Braun
Tim J Brennan
Kit Brown
Stephanie Brown
Sandra Clough
Chet Corey
Sue Crouse
Frances Ann Crowley
Charmaine Pappas
Donovan
Barbara Draper
Neil Dyer
Larry Ellingson
Michael Thomas Ellis
Jeanne Emrich
Sandra Evans
Jeanne Everhart
Michael Forbes
Cindy Fox
Annaliese Gehres
Christy Gove-Berg
Audrae Gruber
Marlys Guimaraes
Kari E Hagstrom
Patrick Cabello Hansel
Laura L Hansen
John Harrington
Sharon Harris

Audrey Kletscher
Helbling
Heidi Hemmer
Jennifer Lundstrom
Hernandez
Mary Willette Hughes
Anne M Jackson
Kristin F Johnson
Linda M Johnson
Celayne Jones
Mim Kagol
James Robert Kane
Paisley Kauffmann
Ryan W Keller
Kathryn Knudson
Susan Koefod
Sonja Kosler
Lynne Maker Kuechle
Ellen Lager
Andrea Taylor
Langworthy
Kim A Larson
Sandra Sidman Larson
Kristin Laurel
Mike Lein
Becky Liestman
Linda Maki
Cheyenne Marco
Margaret M Marty
Susan McMillan
Jerry Mevissen
Rene Montgomery
Colin Murphy

Laura K Murray
David Eric Northington
Vincent D O'Connor
Susan Perala-Dewey
Niomi Rohn Phillips
Shasha C Porter
Adrian S Potter
Rebecca Ramsden
Hosanna Rasmussen
Kit Rohrbach
Deb Schlueter
Ruth Schmidt-Baeumler
Larry Schug
Richard Fenton
Sederstrom
Gene R Stark
Peter William Stein
Doris Lueth Stengel
Thomas C Stetzler
Marlene Mattila Stoehr
Peggy Trojan
Donna Uphus
William Upjohn
Steven R Vogel
Susan Niemela Vollmer
Justin Watkins
Sara Wielenberg
Cheryl Weibye Wilke
Marilyn Wolff
Tarah L Wolff
Lorie Yourd
Kevin Zepper